THE NEGRO AT WORK
DURING THE WORLD WAR
AND DURING RECONSTRUCTION

STATISTICS, PROBLEMS, AND POLICIES RELATING TO
THE GREATER INCLUSION OF NEGRO WAGE EARNERS
IN AMERICAN INDUSTRY AND AGRICULTURE

DIVISION OF NEGRO ECONOMICS
GEORGE E. HAYNES, Ph. D., Director

SECOND STUDY ON NEGRO LABOR

NEGRO UNIVERSITIES PRESS
NEW YORK

Originally published in 1921
by the U.S. Government Printing Office

Reprinted 1969 by
Negro Universities Press
A DIVISION OF GREENWOOD PUBLISHING CORP.
NEW YORK

SBN 0371-1909-X

PRINTED IN UNITED STATES OF AMERICA

CONTENTS.

TABLES.

APPENDIXES.

3

LETTER OF TRANSMITTAL.

UNITED STATES DEPARTMENT OF LABOR,
DIVISION OF NEGRO ECONOMICS,
Washington, D. C., April 1, 1920.

SIR: I have the honor of transmitting herewith a bulletin covering, in brief, some of the work of the Division of Negro Economics, established by you on May 1, 1918, and functioning through your immediate office since that time, together with some valuable data giving the actual experiences of Negroes in industrial occupations, 1918–1919. The publication was planned, in part, by my assistant, Karl F. Phillips, who also constructed the statistical and other tables. contained in the report and who from the beginning and throughout the continuation of the work has given a most competent and highly efficient service to the department and to the public.

You will note that the bulletin contains summarized statements of the policies and plans which you approved for this special service to Negro wage earners, their employers, and associates, and that concise statistical reports and data have been included. The graphs amplifying one of the larger tables were prepared by the Bureau of Labor Statistics. I may say that the files of the Division of Negro Economics contain a mass of similar material, but that owing to lack of funds and clerical help it was not practicable to endeavor to prepare any more material than that which appears in the report.

In transmitting this bulletin I desire to thank the public-spirited citizens, white and colored, in organizations and as individuals, who gave prompt and voluntary assistance of untold value in promoting the work throughout the States and localities in which it was conducted. I desire to thank, also, the Federal, State, and private agencies for their unlimited cooperation and advice at all times. Within the department itself I am grateful to you, to the chiefs and heads of the various divisions and bureaus, and especially to the office of the Assistant Secretary and of the Solicitor for unfailing interest and assistance.

The office and field staff of the division deserves special commendation for untiring zeal and close application in carrying forward the many delicate and difficult tasks growing out of the work almost daily.

I desire again to call your attention to the recommendations cited on pages 134–136 of this bulletin, which, you will recall, were included in my memorandum report to you on the racial situation in Chicago.

Respectfully,

GEORGE E. HAYNES,
Director of Negro Economics.

Hon. W. B. WILSON,
Secretary of Labor.

THE NEGRO AT WORK DURING THE WORLD WAR AND DURING RECONSTRUCTION.

INTRODUCTION.

The entrance of Negroes into industries, particularly in the North during the great war led to many questions: What particular industries did they enter? In what kinds of occupations were they most generally employed? Were they unskilled, semiskilled, or skilled? How did they measure up to the average number of working hours and average earnings as compared with the white workmen? What was the estimate and opinion of employers who tried them? How did they compare with white workmen in the same establishments and on the same jobs as to absenteeism, turn-over, quality of work produced, and speed in turning out quantity?

Some of the chapters of this bulletin bring together the best available data in an attempt to answer some of these questions with the facts. Obviously, the data is very limited in scope and necessarily fragmentary. It would, therefore, be unwise and unscientific to make any large generalizations based upon so limited an amount of data. What is presented, however, has been carefully gathered and collated, and, therefore, gives some definite indications and information where information has been heretofore very limited. Whatever analysis and comment have been made upon the tables and figures may be readily weighed in the light of the accompanying data themselves.

Facts and figures, however, are only bases of information upon which to build programs and plans of action. Negro workers are employed for the most part by white employers and work in the same industries and often on the same jobs with white workers. Their relations with these employers and other workers frequently assume racial as well as labor aspects. In such adjustments as were required during the war, when industries were calling as never before for all kinds of workers, activities which proved successful and valuable in promoting the welfare of these wage-earners and in improving their relations to employers and other workers were exceedingly important parts of the machinery of organized production.

The plans and activities of the Department of Labor for dealing with these matters are experiences of permanent and instructive value, especially because of the hearty and successful response received from white and Negro citizens in many States and localities. A part of this bulletin, therefore, gives a summary of these plans and activities of the Division of Negro Economics in the office of the Secretary of Labor. The account shows the general program, the

7

facts and principles upon which it was based, and how it was carried out in the several States with the hearty indorsement and cooperation of governors and other State and local officials and of white and colored citizens, both in organizations and as individuals.

The first table of figures of Chapter VI gives clear indications of the distribution in 26 States of 129,708 white men and 62,340 Negro men in unskilled occupations of 292 different firms engaged in various war industries in 1918.   Table II of the same chapter gives full details of the classification of occupations as skilled, semiskilled, and unskilled, the average number of hours worked per week, and the average earnings per week and per hour of 4,260 white men and 2,722 Negro men in 194 occupations in 23 separate establishments engaged in basic industrial operations of foundries (both iron and steel), slaughtering and meat packing, automobile manufacture, coke ovens, manufacture of iron and steel and their products, and in glass manufacture.   This table is accompanied by some comment, analyzing the comparison of white and Negro workmen on the points covered in each of the three general occupational classes.   A supplementary part of this table gives similar figures for 153 white women and 83 Negro women in slaughtering and meat packing.   Table III of this chapter gives in tabular form the opinions of 38 employers of Negro workers as to the attitude of their firms toward Negro labor, the opportunities for promotion, and their opinion on the comparative behavior of white and Negro employees.   The 38 firms represented were employing at that time 108,215 white workers and 6,757 Negro workers.·   These opinions, therefore, are fairly representative of the state of mind of northern employers in 1918–19.

Slaughtering and meat packing and iron and steel were such important industries and employed such large numbers of Negroes during the war that special reports were secured through courtesy of plants carrying on these two industries.   Chapter VII gives in considerable detail the tables and analyses of white and Negro workers for the first of these industries and adds additional discussion to that of Chapter VI on the iron and steel establishments.

Tables IV and V of this chapter give the number and per cent of distribution of the white and Negro employees, male and female, of two slaughtering and meat-packing plants for 30 weeks beginning July 13, 1918, and 159 weeks beginning January, 1916, respectively. On the basis of these tables two diagrams have been made and are included in the chapter, making these figures of the total numbers and percentages readily perceptible to the casual reader.   There was no more important nor interesting work than that in the shipyards during the war.   "Ships, ships, and more ships" was the call from Europe.   It has not been feasible to get all the figures for all the shipyards where Negroes were employed during the war, but a full record of the Negro employees at shipbuilding plants under the jurisdiction of the United States Shipping Board, Emergency Fleet Corporation, were secured through courtesy of that board.   This activity of Negro wage-earners assumed such important proportions that the material justifies a separate chapter—Chapter VIII.   Table VI of this chapter gives these figures for occupations of 24,648 Negro men during the war and 14,075 after the war and until September, 1919. They are classified both as a whole into skilled and unskilled and by specific occupations for each of the eight shipyard districts under the

Emergency Fleet Corporation. Some analysis of the figures given in this chapter indicates their significance.

Unfortunately this study of Negro wage-earners does not include data of their labor on the railroads, in the mines, in agriculture, and in domestic service, except as some of these are included in some of the figures given in the several tables below, and in the State reports of activities of the State supervisors of Negro Economics, notably in Chapter XVI on Ohio, in Chapter X on Illinois, in Chapter XII on Mississippi, and in Chapter XV on North Carolina.

The original plan for this bulletin contemplated the inclusion of these groups. The activities of the department embraced measures to promote their welfare, their efficiency, and to improve their relations and opportunities. During this study efforts were made without satisfactory results to get comprehensive figures and facts from the United States Railroad Administration on this subject because their figures were not compiled separately. Figures for the other groups also could not be obtained from any available sources. There were not funds at hand for the Department of Labor to study these occupational groups with a staff of its own. It was deemed best, therefore, to await further provision for such study rather than attempt to include uncertain statements and insufficient and inexact data. The experience of the department in touching these fields demonstrates their importance and justifies this postponement until they can be properly studied.

Special note should be made of the sincere and effective cooperation of Mr. Ethelbert Stewart, Director of the Investigation and Inspection Service, whose staff workers were directed so effectively in the collection of a considerable amount of the statistical data included in several of the chapters.

The Women's Bureau (formerly the Woman in Industry Service), first under Miss Mary Van Kleeck as director and now under Miss Mary Anderson as director, has given effective attention to the questions affecting Negro women workers in industry and their relations to white women workers. During the war Mrs. Helen B. Irvin, as special agent of the Woman in Industry Service, assisted a part of the time by Mrs. Elizabeth R. Haynes as a dollar-a-year worker, made visits and inspections of a number of establishments that were employing Negro women. A summary of Mrs. Irvin's reports about firms employing approximately 21,547 Negro women and girls is given in Chapter XIX. This discussion gives the general kind of industrial and other work in which these women were employed, indicates some of the problems arising out of their entrance in large numbers into such work, and describes some of the typical conditions under which they labored.

The records of the activities of the State supervisors of Negro Economics speak for themselves in Chapters IX to XVIII. The men in the field who followed the series of conferences and supervised on the ground the formation of State and local Negro workers' advisory committees in the counties, towns, and cities of 11 States, with the necessary local routine to make effective the cooperation of white and colored citizens in meeting their many difficult and delicate racial labor problems, deserve high commendation as volunteer officers in the third line of defense in industry and agriculture which labored to make the world safe for democracy.

CHAPTER I.

MIGRATION.

Shortage of labor in northern industries was the direct cause of the increased Negro migration during the war period. This direct cause was, of course, augmented by other causes, among which were the increased dissatisfaction with conditions in the South—the ravages of the boll weevil, floods, change of crop system, low wages, and poor houses and schools.

A previous bulletin of the department summed up the causes as follows:

Other causes assigned at the southern end are numerous: General dissatisfaction with conditions, ravages of boll weevil, floods, change of crop system, low wages, poor houses on plantations, poor school facilities, unsatisfactory crop settlements, rough treatment, lynching, desire for travel, labor agents, the Negro press, letters from friends in the North, and finally advice of white friends in the South where crops had failed.

The Department of Labor estimates the Negro migration in figures of from 400,000 to 500,000. Other estimates, ranging from 300,000 to 800,000, have been made by individual experts and by private bureaus. Such a variation of figures goes to show the wide scope of the migration. Prior to the war period the Negro worker had been sparsely located in the North, but the laws of self-preservation of the industrial and agricultural assets of our country and the law of demand and supply turned almost overnight both into war and private industries hundreds of thousands of Negro workers, among whom there were laborers, molders, carpenters, blacksmiths, painters, janitors, chauffeurs, machinist laborers, and a mass of other workers, comprising, probably, nearly every type of skilled, semiskilled, and unskilled labor.

The most marked effects of the migration were easily determinable. First, the agricultural regions of the Southern States, particularly Mississippi and Louisiana, began to suffer for want of the Negro worker who had so long tilled the soil of those regions. On the other hand, the Negro workers who had been turned into the plants of the North faced the necessity of performing efficient work in the minimum amount of time, of adjusting themselves to northern conditions and of becoming fixtures in their particular line of employment, or becoming "floaters."

It is interesting to review for a moment some of the wage scales in Southern States. In 1917 about $12 a month was being paid for farm labor in many sections. In other sections 75 cents and $1 a day were considered equitable wages. During the harvesting of rice in the "grinding season" the amount was usually increased to $1.25 and $1.75 per day, with a possible average of $1.50. Cotton was always considered a cheap-labor crop, about which one man has said:

The world has gone on thinking that the farm labor in the South should work for 75 cents or $1 a day when all other labor is getting $1.50 and $2 per day.

The States which contributed most largely to the masses of migrants were North Carolina, South Carolina, Florida, Alabama, Mississippi, Louisiana, Texas, Arkansas, and Tennessee. The migrants from those States rapidly supplemented the Negro workers already sparsely employed in Pennsylvania, New Jersey, Michigan, Illinois, and West Virginia.[1]

---

[1] See Negro Migration in 1916–17, Department of Labor bulletin. Government Printing Office. 1919.

CHAPTER II.

CREATION OF THE OFFICE OF DIRECTOR OF NEGRO ECONOMICS.

In view of the perplexing questions with regard to Negroes in industry and agriculture and the migration of Negroes from the South to the North during 1916, 1917, and 1918, upon representations of white and Negro citizens and several influential organizations dealing particularly with Negro life and race relations, the Secretary of Labor, Hon. William B. Wilson, after consideration and favorable recommendation by his Advisory Council on the war organization of the Department of Labor, decided to create the position of adviser on Negro labor in his immediate office, with the title of Director of Negro Economics. The function of this official was to advise the Secretary and the directors and chiefs of the several bureaus and divisions of the department on matters relating to Negro wage earners, and to outline and promote plans for greater cooperation between Negro wage earners, white employers, and white workers in agriculture and industry.

In starting this work the Secretary stated that as Negroes constitute about one-tenth of the total population of the country and about one-seventh of the working population, it was reasonable and right that they should have representation at the council table when matters affecting them were being considered and decided. In defining the function of the office of the Director of Negro Economics the Secretary decided that the advice of the director should be secured before any work dealing with Negro wage earners was undertaken and that he be kept advised of the progress of such work so that the Department might have, at all times, the benefit of his judgment in all matters affecting Negroes.

Accordingly, on May 1, 1918, the Secretary of Labor called to that position Dr. George E. Haynes, professor of sociology and economics at Fisk University and one of the secretaries of the National League on Urban Conditions among Negroes. Dr. Haynes was strongly recommended by many individuals and organizations, among them being the Commercial Club of Nashville, Tenn., his home city.

The Secretary of Labor, with the advice of the Director of Negro Economics, early in May, 1918, considered and approved plans outlining three types of activities for dealing with problems of Negro workers in their relations to white workers and white employers, as follows:

1. The organization of cooperative committees of white and colored citizens in the States and localities where problems of Negro labor arise, due to large numbers of Negro workers.

2. The development of a publicity or educational campaign to create good feeling between the races and to have both white and Negro citizens understand and cooperate with the purpose and plans of the department.

12

3. The appointment of Negro staff workers in the States and localities to develop this organization of committees, to conduct this work of better racial labor relations, and to assist the several divisions and services of the department in mobilizing and stabilizing Negro labor for winning the war.

In undertaking to carry out the three parts of this plan, the office of the Secretary recognized two main difficulties:

1. The difficulty of forestalling a strong feeling of suspicion on the part of the colored people, growing out of their past experiences in racial and labor matters.

2. The difficulty of forestalling a wrong impression among white people, especially those in the South, about the efforts of the department, and of having them understand that the department wishes to help them in local labor problems by means of its plans.

These cardinal facts were also given due consideration:

1. The two races are thrown together in their daily work, the majority of the employers and a large number of the employees having relations with Negro employees being white persons. These conditions give rise to misunderstandings, prejudices, antagonisms, fears, and suspicions. These facts must be recognized and dealt with in a statesmanlike manner.

2. The problems are local in character, arising, as they do, between local employers and local employees. The people, however, in local communities, need the vision of national policies, plans, and standards to apply to their local situations.

3. Any plan or program should be based upon the desire and need of cooperation between white employers and representatives of Negro wage earners, and, wherever possible, white wage earners.

FIELD ORGANIZATION—CONFERENCES AND COMMITTEES.

The first step in setting up the field organization was a preliminary trip of the Director of Negro Economics to strategic centers in a number of States where Negro workers' problems were of pressing importance. Through preliminary correspondence, informal conferences and interviews were held with representative white and Negro citizens from different parts of each State visited. These interviews and conferences established the first points of sympathetic contact for cooperation in subsequent efforts to improve labor conditions and race relations.

These preliminary visits laid the foundation for subsequent work. For instance, the North Carolina conference, called by Hon. T. W. Bickett, Governor of the State and described below, which set the model for other Southern States, grew out of such a preliminary visit. The creation of the Negro workers' committees of Virginia and the cooperation of the Negro Organization Society of that State grew out of a similar visit on the trip. Similar results followed the connections made in other States.

Upon the visit to a State, officials of State and private schools for Negroes, of the State councils of defense, representatives of the chambers of commerce, of the United States Employment Service, and of white and Negro colleges promised cooperation and assistance in the efforts of the department to stimulate Negro wage earners by improving their condition in such a way as to increase their efficiency for maximum production to win the war.

The first of a series of State conferences of representative white and Negro citizens was called on June 19, 1918, by Hon. T. W. Bickett, Governor of North Carolina, at his office in the State capitol at Raleigh. There were present at this conference 17 of the most substantial Negroes from all parts of the State and five white citizens, including the governor, who presided throughout the conference and took an active part in the proceedings.

The plans of the Department of Labor for increasing the morale and efficiency of Negro workers were outlined by the Director of Negro Economics and freely discussed. At the close of the meeting the governor appointed a temporary committee which drafted a constitution providing for a State Negro Workers' Advisory Committee and for the organization of local county and city committees. This plan of organization, with slight modifications and readjustments, later served as a model for other States in the development of a voluntary field organization which was set up in the course of the next six months in four other southern States, and six northern States. Gov. Bickett was so highly pleased with the result of the conference that he issued a statement to the public press saying that this meeting was one of the most patriotic and helpful conferences he had ever attended.

A State meeting of white and colored citizens was held by the Southern Sociological Congress at Gulfport, Miss., July 12, 1918. The congress extended an invitation to the Director of Negro Economics to address the meeting. About 200 white citizens, business men and planters, and about 75 Negro citizens of the State were in attendance. The department took advantage of this State gathering to call together those who were especially interested in the adjustment of Negro labor problems. The address of the Director of Negro Economics before the congress received a hearty response from both whites and Negroes present, and as a result several of the white citizens took an active part in the conference, which worked out a plan of State-wide organization similar to the one adopted by North Carolina.

On the basis of the precedent set by Gov. Bickett and the success at the Gulfport meeting of the Southern Sociological Congress, Hon. Sidney Catts, Governor of Florida, called a conference of white and Negro citizens at Jacksonville, on July 16, 1918. After full discussion of plans and procedure this conference adopted a program and formed a State Negro Workers' Advisory Committee composed of representative white and colored citizens under the auspices of the State Council of National Defense and the United States Employment Service. A program of activities was worked out, having as its object the promotion of better conditions and a better understanding of employment matters relating to the Negroes of Florida in order that greater production of food and war supplies might be the result. So great was the enthusiasm on the day of the conference that the citizens of Jacksonville, white and colored, held a monster mass meeting, at which the governor, the Director of Negro Economics, and other officials spoke.

In the meantime, through the help of the Negro Organization Society of Virginia, the Negro Workers' Advisory Committee of that State was organized and the first supervisor of Negro economics, a Negro citizen of training and experience, T. C. Erwin, was appointed and undertook the direction of advisory work in the State.

The next step was to get the work and organization launched in northern territory. Ohio was selected for the initial effort, and on August 5, 1918, a conference was called by the department with the hearty help of the Federal Director of the United States Employment

Service and Hon. James M. Cox, governor of Ohio. This conference met at the State Capitol at Columbus and was notable for the number in attendance, and the enthusiasm and readiness with which they worked out a plan of State-wide organization. There were present about 125 persons—white employers, Negro wage earners, and representatives of white wage earners. The afternoon session was closed with a splendid address by the governor. The conference adopted the usual plan of State organization and Charles E. Hall, the second supervisor of Negro economics, was assigned to the State to develop the organization and to supervise the work, under the auspices of the United States Employment Service office.

One other conference, that held in Louisville, Ky., August 6, 1918, needs to be described as showing one other slight variation in the far-reaching significance of the cooperative plan of organization. This conference was unique in that the plan of organization adopted was that of a united war-work committee made up jointly by those representing the State Council of Defense, United States Food Administration, United States Department of Agriculture, and the United States Department of Labor, white and colored citizens being the persons representing these various interests. The conference was noted for its enthusiasm. Hon. A. O. Stanley, governor of Kentucky, made an enthusiastic address to the conference and a large mass meeting followed in the evening.

By the time of the Kentucky conference, three months after the first plans were outlined, the influence of the State conferences and their feasibility were so well proved as a means of starting a State movement and creating good will and favorable sentiment that other conferences followed as a matter of course in setting up the State work. Additional conferences in 1918 were held in Georgia, Missouri, Illinois, Michigan, and New Jersey.

A national informal conference was called by the Secretary of Labor and met in Washington, D. C., February 17–18, 1919. This conference included men and women representing welfare and social service organizations, both North and South, of both Negroes and white people, in order that the views and interests of all sections and of both races might be ascertained. The keynote of the conference was sounded by the Secretary of Labor in welcoming the representatives. He said:

Congress in defining the duties of the Department of Labor made no distinction either as to sex or race, and, I may add, as to previous condition of servitude. We were authorized to promote the welfare of wage earners, whether men or women or children, whether they were white or colored, whether they were native born or alien residents; and in the undertaking to promote the welfare of the wage workers we have not assumed that it was our duty to promote the welfare of the wageworker at the expense of the plans of the community but to promote the welfare of the wageworker, having due respect to the rights of all other portions of our population.

The Assistant Secretary of Labor, Louis F. Post, in addressing the conference said:

It is the function of the Department of Labor to look after the interests of all wage earners of any race, any age, or either sex.

Special subjects were discussed, as follows:

Lines of work which should be undertaken for improving race relations and conditions of Negro workers.

Conduct and toleration as necessary for cooperation and good will between Negro
and white workers.

Special problems of women in industry.

The Negro land tenants and farm laborers and what agencies may do to help them.

Education and Negro workers.

On the second day the informal conference gave most of its time
to the general topic: "Unity of action in local communities to secure
efficiency and cooperation of welfare agencies and methods, by
which the Department of Labor and other governmental agencies
can best cooperate with private agencies and organizations."

In a set of resolutions adopted and recommended to the Secretary
of Labor the following important points are set forth:

**RESOLUTION ON PLAN OF COOPERATIVE ORGANIZATION ADOPTED AT INFORMAL CON-
FERENCE ON NEGRO LABOR PROBLEMS, FEBRUARY 17 AND 18, 1919, AS APPROVED
BY THE SECRETARY OF LABOR.**

Whereas the improvement of conditions of Negro wage earners and the improvement
of relations of white employers, of white wage earners and of Negro wage earners are
questions of great importance for the advancement of the welfare of all wage earners
in America; and

Whereas the several organizations and agencies specifically interested in promoting
the better adjustment of Negro wage earners to American life need to work in closer
cooperation:

Therefore, It behooves representatives of such boards, agencies and organizations
interested in such questions to adopt measures of cooperative organization, of action,
and of policy that will foster constructive work along these lines.

We, therefore, the representatives of such organizations, invited to an informal conference in Washington by the Secretary of Labor, do hereby recommend and ask the
Secretary to use his good offices in laying before the organizations represented, and
any other organizations that may be interested, a plan of cooperative organization and
effort on the following general lines:

1. That local efforts to influence employers of Negro workers to provide welfare
facilities be undertaken, jointly, by all the agencies attempting to do such work in a
community; and that the local representatives of the Department of Labor be used as
far as practicable as a channel through which the experiences and methods of the several agencies shall seek exchange in these local efforts.

Where there is no such local governmental organization or representative of the
Department of Labor, and several agencies desire to act, that they request the Department of Labor to assist them in getting such a neutral channel of cooperation.

2. That our several agencies, boards and organizations, which undertake the organization of any work or the expenditure of any funds for improving the living and neighborhood conditions of Negro workers in local communities seek to become informed of
similar plans of other agencies, boards and organizations before deciding on plans or
taking action.

3. That the Department of Labor be asked to furnish such information and to
provide such facilities as are necessary for keeping the agencies, boards and organizations informed of such plans, efforts, or proposed undertakings or steps that have been
undertaken by the several agencies, boards and organizations interested.

4. That each agency, board or organization here represented, or any other agency,
board or organization that may hereafter be concerned shall, as soon as practicable,
make available to the Department of Labor such parts of its records, facilities and
opportunities as are necessary in order that the Department may have available the
information needed for using its good offices in furthering the cooperation of such agencies, boards, or organizations. That such agencies, boards, or organizations detail for
service in this connection such personnel services of its staff as may be needed for
carrying out the part of any effort in which said agency, board, or organization may be
involved.

5. The Department of Labor is also asked to call a second conference, at the time
that seems best, of representatives of the organizations that have been invited to this
conference; also representatives of such other organizations that may be interested or
concerned for futher discussion of the questions involved in connection with Negro
economics, in order that further exchange of experiences and plans of unity and cooperation may be discussed

The following resolution was adopted by the conference as an addition to the report of the committee:

6. That it is the consensus of this body that the representatives of national organizations attending this conference request their local representatives in various States to cooperate immediately with the representatives of the Director of Negro Economics of the United States Department of Labor in all matters affecting the interests of the Negro workers.

A program of national work was also adopted and recommended to the Secretary covering the following matters:

1. Survey of Negro labor conditions.
2. The getting of Negro workers into industry.
3. Holding Negro workers in industry, including the improving of living and working conditions in both agriculture and industry.
4. Training the next generation of workers.
5. The general advancement of Negro wage earners in the United States.

The following are some of the organizations signing, and the names of their representatives:

Name.	Organization or agency represented.
Dr. Jesse E. Moorland (chairman)	International Committee, Y. M. C. A.
(Miss) Nannie Burroughs	The National Training School.
(Miss) Mary C. Jackson	War Work Council, Y. W. C. A. (National Board).
John R. Shillady	}National Association for the Advancement of Colored People.
(Vice) Walter F. White	
T. S. Settle	War Camp Community Service.
Eugene Kinckle Jones	National League on Urban Conditions among Negroes.
Dr. Thomas Jesse Jones	Phelp-Stokes Fund.
C. H. Tobias	National War Work Council, Y. M. C. A.
John T. Emlen	Armstrong Association of Philadelphia.
Dr. Rodney W. Roundy	American Missionary Association.
Dr. R. R. Moton	Tuskegee Institute.
Rev. Harold M. Kingsley	Joint Committee, War Production Committees.
Rev. E. W. Moore	Baptist Home Mission Society.
(Mrs.) Etnah R. Bouttee	Circle for Negro War Relief (Inc.).
(Miss) Estelle Haskin	Women's Home Mission Council—Methodist Publishing Board.
John J. Eagan	Commission on Training Camp Activities.
Dr. James H. Dillard	Jeanes-Slater Funds.

In carrying out the plans for a publicity and educational campaign to create a better feeling between the races and to have both white and colored citizens understand and cooperate with the purposes and plans of the department, the office of the Director of Negro Economics received the hearty help and cooperation of the Information and Education Service of the department during the war and until that service was discontinued July 1, 1919.

A regular newspaper release was given to both the white press and Negro press which can not be too highly commended for their cooperation. Special mention should be made of the support given by the Negro newspapers of the country, more than 250 in number, who gave without compensation large sections of news columns and advertising space. As an illustration, a news release on that part of the Secretary's annual report relating to Negro workers was sent out from the office of the Director of Negro Economics through the Information and Education Service. Clippings from white newspapers showed that the release was used by them as far north as Maine, as far west as California, and as far south as Louisiana. Nearly all the Negro newspapers, north and south, carried the release—some of them in full.

Special addresses for use at patriotic and holiday celebrations were prepared and sent out to the Negro workers through the advisory committees in the territories where they were organized.   On the Fourth of July, 1918, more than 2,000 copies of an address entitled "Labor and Victory" were used in county and city patriotic celebrations in more than 150 counties and about 12 States.   (For copy, see Appendix I.)

Statements were prepared for writers of special articles in newspapers and magazines and for the Four Minute Bulletin of the Committee on Public Information.   Similar material was sent to hundreds of speakers in different parts of the country.   Magazine articles dealing with the problems of Negro labor during the war and reconstruction and the work of the Division of Negro Economics were prepared and appeared in such magazines as The American Review of Reviews, The Crisis, The Public, and The Survey.

The United States Public Health Service in its effort to combat venereal diseases inaugurated a special effort to reach all Negroes. This office cooperated with the Public Health Service by helping that service to get in touch with Negro workers through our field organization in order that they might become acquainted with the facts relative to disease as it affected health and efficiency.

The Negro workers' advisory committees organized and held many public meetings, attended by both white and colored citizens, to discuss the problems of labor and the war.   Speakers were sent to hundreds of other meetings.   We estimate that each month no less than a million Negro workers and hundreds of employers were reached and influenced in this way.

CHAPTER III.

EARLY RESULTS OF NEGRO ECONOMICS SERVICE.

At the end of the first six months of the work, Negro workers' advisory committees, by States, counties, and cities, had been wholly or partly formed in 11 States, and by the time the armistice was signed steps had been taken to establish committees in three other States.

Nearly all of these committees, both State and local, had white and Negro members or had cooperating white members representing organizations of white employers and white workers. In all, 11 State committees and about 225 local county and city committees, with a membership numbering more than 1,000, were appointed. One of the most remarkable facts is that out of the invitations and acceptances for service of all of these white and colored persons on these committees, so far as we have any record, there was only one case of a member of one committee whose relationship on the committee caused friction and made necessary a request for his resignation. There was the heartiest response from citizens of both races everywhere. Many of them used large amounts of time, gave their services, and often spent their own money to further the departmental program. It was the expressed opinion of many citizens of well-known competence that the holding of these conferences and the voluntary cooperation of hundreds of white and Negro citizens on these committees, both north and south, were in themselves sufficient to justify all the effort put forth by the department. Even more significant were the many written statements of commendation from citizens in all parts of the country and from organizations that cooperated and helped in the movement.

SELECTION AND TRAINING OF A STAFF.

The selection and training of a staff for such work ordinarily would hardly be considered as one of the results of a departmental or organization effort. However, it should be borne in mind that there is usually serious doubt about the expert efficiency of Negroes in official positions which call for high standards of character and ability. Often criticism has been specially lodged against Negroes in public office. Therefore, the successful and effective selection and organization of a staff of Negro officials and employees, with the necessary general training, expert knowledge, and experience to carry out the program of work and to achieve the results as shown in the succeeding pages, was in itself an achievement.

This work of mediation between white workers, white employers, and Negro workers called for exceptional qualities of mind and character in addition to technical knowledge and efficiency. The spirit of conciliation and cooperation, the ability to see both sides of any issue, and the combination of initiative and self-control necessary to act effectively when action is called for and to wait with patience when action is not strategic required persons far above the average in both character and ability.   The office of the Director of Negro Economics may modestly claim this success as a part of the achievement of the work, as it demonstrates that such a staff can be built up in the public service.

The department had previously used the services of three Negro experts from the Department of Commerce.   These men were retained and their duties readjusted so that throughout the period of the war and for nearly eight months of reconstruction they gave effective service—Charles E. Hall as supervisor of Negro economics for Ohio, William Jennifer as supervisor of Negro economics for Michigan, and Harry E. Arnold as an examiner and special agent in the United States Employment Service in Pennsylvania.   As the organization grew, the following men were added: T. C. Erwin, supervisor of Negro economics for Virginia; Dr. A. M. Moore, supervisor of Negro economics for North Carolina, who served as a dollar-a-year man, with R. McCants Andrews as assistant; William M. Ashby, supervisor of Negro economics for New Jersey; W. O. Armwood, supervisor of Negro economics for Florida; Lemuel L. Foster, supervisor of Negro economics for Mississippi, who succeeded J. C. Olden, resigned for other work after doing valuable service; H. A. Hunt, supervisor of Negro economics for Georgia; and Forrester B. Washington, supervisor of Negro economics for Illinois.   In addition, the qualifications and recommendations of a number of Negro examiners in the United States Employment Service, as well as stenographers and clerical assistants, were investigated and passed upon by the office of the Director of Negro Economics.

In the office of the Director of Negro Economics at Washington headquarters, Karl F. Phillips, as assistant to the director, ably managed the office and closely associated with the director in the full supervision of the work.   A competent staff of clerical employees was added as the growth of the work made it necessary.

These Federal officials performed their duties with enthusiasm, efficiency, and success under the many trying circumstances which arose during the strenuous months of the war labor program and the first months of reconstruction.   Their services as a part of this experiment in the Federal Government's relation to Negro wage earners has been a contribution to the experience with Negroes in important administrative positions.

The facts about each State supervisor of Negro economics follow in sections describing the activities and results of the work in each State.

PROBLEMS OF NEGRO LABOR.

Before entering the detailed discussion of migration and the experiences in 11 States, a summarized statement of the problems of Negro labor during the war and reconstruction period, extracted from reports of the Director of Negro Economics to the Secretary of Labor, follows:

I. During the war period.

    1. The movement of large numbers of Negro workers from the South to the North.

    2. The inevitable maladjustment in living conditions confronting the newcomers in the North.

3. The delicate questions of relations of Negro workers and white workers in northern industries into which Negroes were for the first time entering in large numbers.
4. The difficulties and readjustments in southern agricultural regions, due to the sudden departure of thousands of tenants and farm laborers, as well as the readjustments in industrial operations in the South, due to the same causes.
5. The attraction to centers of war industries and construction camps and cantonments, both north and south, due to the wages offered, which were higher than those prevailing in post-war industry and agriculture.
6. The serious labor shortage, both north and south, white and colored, due to the drafting of millions of men into the Army.

II. During the reconstruction period.

1. The thousands of Negro workers in war industries who had to be shifted back to post war industries along with the other workers called for special attention similar to the period when they were being shifted into war industries.
2. Probably between 400,000 and 500,000 workers migrated from the South to northern industries. The difficulties of cooperative adjustment of white wage earners and Negro wage earners in the industrial communities where they must find community life in contact with each other were increased.
3. Special problems connected with the entrance of colored women into industry and special problems in domestic and personal service.
4. The problems of improving the conditions, increasing the efficiency, and encouraging the thrift of Negro workers were probably greater during the war and still remain as reconstruction problems.
5. In the South the common interests of white employers who want to engage the services which the Negro wage earner has to offer and the desire of the worker for wages in return make the adjustment of the Negro labor situation one of the most far-reaching factors in bringing about just and amicable race relations. The migration and war restlessness of the two races creates problems which the labor nexus may be very effective in settling.
6. The adjustment of farm tenantry and of the labor situation in the South is very largely a problem of Negro labor.
7. For the first 12 months following the armistice the problem of demobilization of thousands of Negro soldiers called for cooperative action, and more tact and judgment than were probably needed during the period when they were being drafted out of production into the Army. The return of the Negro soldier to civil life, with the obligations of the Nation to him, has been one of the most delicate and difficult labor questions confronting the Nation, north and south.
8. The improvement of living and working conditions, including such questions as housing, sanitation, and recreation of Negro wage earners, should receive more attention during this period of reconstruction and peace time than they did before or during the Great War period.

CHAPTER IV.

COOPERATION WITH THE SEVERAL BUREAUS AND DIVISIONS OF THE DEPARTMENT.

Where matters which manifestly or directly affected Negro wage earners came under the immediate administrative guidance of the several divisions and bureaus of the department, it was the plan of the Secretary that the heads or chiefs of such divisions or bureaus should call upon the Director of Negro Economics for advice.

The United States Employment Service, which was dealing with the recruiting and placing of Negro labor in the United States, naturally received the largest amount of such cooperation, advice, and planning. For instance, questions came up relating to private agencies and their handling of Negro labor on and after August 1, 1918, when the Employment Service was given the responsibility of recruiting and placing the common labor in war industries employing 100 or more workers. The Director of Negro Economics gathered the facts and proposed a plan and policy for dealing with this matter. Such plan and policy were later adopted and put into operation by the Director General of the United States Employment Service.

The members of the Negro workers' advisory committees in many localities assisted as volunteers during this war-labor recruiting and placing. Eight of the State supervisiors of Negro economics had their offices either with the Federal directors of the Employment Service or in close connection with them. All of the Federal directors in these States turned to these State supervisors for advice and assistance on practically all matters relating to the handling of Negro labor in their States. The question of location of offices to serve Negro neighborhoods, the formation of policies and plans of the Employment Service to serve them more effectively, the selection of competent Negro examiners, and a number of other questions were from time to time presented and handled for the Employment Service. The following excerpts from statements of some of the Federal directors of the Employment Service show their appreciation of this service given by representatives of the Division of Negro Economics:

UNITED STATES EMPLOYMENT SERVICE.

74 East Gay Street, Columbus, Ohio, April 9, 1919.

Mr. ETHELBERT STEWART,
Director of Investigation and Inspection Service,
Office of the Secretary, Department of Labor, Washington, D. C.

MY DEAR MR. STEWART: Mr. Charles E. Hall, who has been supervisor of Negro economics in Ohio, handed me a copy of your letter of March 27 with reference to his reports being made through the office of the Federal director for Ohio.

Mr. Hall has been located in the office of the Federal director for the past several months and we are very glad to advise that the relationship is very pleasant. We feel that Mr. Hall is a very competent man and especially fitted for the line of work to which he is assigned.

This letter is written as an acknowledgment of the receipt of instructions contained in your letter of above date.

Very truly, yours,

(Signed)   C. H. MAYHUGH,
Acting Federal Director for Ohio.

1423 NEWTON STREET, *Washington, D. C., July 9, 1919.*

Dr. GEORGE E. HAYNES,
  Director of Negro Economics, Department of Labor, Washington, D. C.

MY DEAR DR. HAYNES: I very much regret to learn that failure of appropriation has made it necessary to discontinue the work which has been carried on by Mr. Charles E. Hall, supervisor of Negro economics for Ohio.

Mr. Hall assisted the Employment Service in every possible way in recruiting labor during the war and in the readjustment of labor after the signing of the armistice.

The big task before him at this time is to assist in crystallizing the best thought and carrying out the best possible plans for improving housing conditions and aiding the Negroes to become satisfactorily adjusted to the new industrial condition which confronts them. His work, I believe, has been a real factor in preventing the development of radical unrest among the Negroes in Ohio.

My knowledge of Mr. Hall's work was gained through contact as Federal Director of Employment for Ohio, from which position I resigned March 15, 1919.

Very truly, yours,

(Signed)   FRED C. CROXTON.

UNITED STATES EMPLOYMENT SERVICE,
Meridian, Miss., January 29, 1919.

From: Federal director.
To: Director General.
Subject: Negro Economics Division.

1. In replying to letter from Assistant Director General, dated January 23, in reference to Division of Negro Economics.

2. In this connection the writer wishes to state that this service is providing an office on the same floor as the office of the Federal director for the supervisor of Negro economics. The present supervisor, L. L. Foster, a young Negro of energy, is conferring almost daily with the Federal director in reference to his work.

3. The writer attended the meeting of the Negro State advisory board in Jackson, Monday, January 27, at which meeting plans were perfected for the organization of the Negro boys between the ages of 16 and 21 in Mississippi in the Boys' Working Reserve. Cooperation has been obtained from the State agriculture college, and they have agreed to supply instructors wherever necessary to instruct these Negro boys in a short course prepared by the Reserve. Arrangements were made for visiting and organizing reserves in approximately twenty industrial Negro schools in the State for the giving of this course in connection with these schools in the early spring. This Service will then undertake to place these students in active farm work as soon as school is closed.

4. The Negro workers' advisory committee in the State of Mississippi is well organized and the work is prospering very satisfactorily.

(Signed)   H. H. WEIR,
Federal Director.

DETROIT, MICH, *July 2, 1919.*

From: Federal director.
To: Director General, United States Employment Service, Washington, D. C.
Subject: Supervisor of Negro Economics for Michigan.

1. On Thursday of last week Mr. William Jennifer, who for the past nine months has been acting as supervisor of Negro economics for Michigan, advised me that he was in receipt of communication from Washington directing him to report there immediately. He left here on Friday morning, and at the time of his leaving stated that he was somewhat worried in regards to the work, which he had been carrying on here in Michigan, being continued.

2. At the time Mr. Jennifer came to Michigan he at once proceeded to develop the State, and within a short time after his arrival a conference was held here in Detroit, and there was in attendance representatives from 19 different cities in Michigan. An organization was perfected at that time, and great good has come from the results of that meeting. The writer attended this conference and had an opportunity to meet with these representatives, who consisted of ministers, doctors, lawyers, welfare workers, and workingmen. These people went back to their respective localities and proceeded to enlighten the colored people of their community regarding the efforts being made by the Government to assist them in caring for the interests of the Negroes who are rapidly moving here from the Southern States.

3. It would appear to the writer that there is no work of greater importance which the Government might be interested in at this time than that or assisting the colored people to bring about better conditions for their race.

4. Since coming to Michigan, Mr. Jennifer has worked hard and given to the duties assigned to him all his time and efforts. He is a splendid gentleman and his heart is in his work. He thoroughly understands the Negro problem. In the mind of the writer, he is an exception to the average person, and we should very much like to see him return to Michigan to carry on this good work which he has been doing, and desire to urge upon you the importance of this department being continued.

(Signed)   J. V. Cunningham,
Federal Director.

United States Employment Service,
9 Franklin Street, Newark, N. J., April 2, 1919.

Prof. George E. Haynes,
Director of Negro Economics, Washington, D. C.

My Dear Dr. Haynes: It is my understanding that you desire an expression of opinion as to the work of the Bureau of Negro Economics.

I am glad to inform you that it is our understanding that Negro advisory committees have been organized in the principal industrial centers throughout the State. Those committees hold regular meetings at which Mr. Ashby (supervisor of Negro economics for New Jersey) is often present and he addresses these groups on matters relative to the situation pertaining to Negro labor in the State and advises them as to how they can make the best of their opportunities. Committees of this character have been helpful in the offices in the matter of opportunities for colored men and women, and also in molding sentiment in favor of colored workers.

The Camden (N. J.) committee is doing an especially fine piece of work in the interest of the returning colored soldiers. Mr. Ashby personally attends the meetings of the welfare organizations wherever it is possible in the State, giving specific attention to the benefits that may accrue to the colored workers.

Personally, I can only speak in the highest terms of the work which he has been enabled to accomplish for the benefit of the Negro workers of New Jersey. I feel quite satisfied that, responsive to the energetic work which he has performed, various colored organizations throughout the State found it advisable for their best interests to send telegrams to the various Washington representatives asking for continuation of the United States Employment Service.

Very truly, yours,

(Signed)   J. Spitz,
Assistant Federal Director of Employment for New Jersey.

Also, in Virginia and Alabama service of cooperation was given to the Boys' Working Reserve in assisting its representatives in those States to secure helpful contacts with Negro boys.

When the Women's Bureau was established in the department, it was natural that its scope of activities should include attention to conditions affecting colored women workers and that this bureau should counsel and work closely with the office of the Director of Negro Economics, which gave assistance not only in finding and selecting Mrs. Helen B. Irvin as industrial agent for the work among colored women, and in securing Mrs. Elizabeth Ross Haynes (as a dollar-a-year employee) for the direction of the same work, but also in making surveys of Negro women in industrial establishments and in taking other steps for improvement of working conditions and relations of Negro women in industry, carried out in joint cooperation with that service. (For full summary of reports see section on "Negro Women in industry," pp. 124–133.)

These experts entered upon their duties in November, 1918. They performed important field service of a varied character, and the data collected by them, together with their recommendations, after receiving the counsel and advice of the Director of Negro Economics, formed the basis of concrete labor policies which the Women's Bureau is now putting into effect in behalf of female Negro workers. Some of the facts gathered are published in another section of this bulletin.

The Investigation and Inspection Service not only made a number of investigations of plants of various kinds involved in the department relating to Negro wage earners but this service took upon itself the employment of a competent Negro, Byron K. Armstrong, who was also associated with the office of the Director of Negro Economics. The field investigations for the data in Chapters VIII and X, which deal with Negroes in the seven basic industries in northern centers were made by him and other representatives of that service in an effort to ascertain the conditions and relations obtaining between Negro workmen who had entered northern industries and white workers.

Special mention should be made of the cooperation received from the Council of National Defense in starting and developing a program for Negro workers in the South. The national office of the council, at Washington, D. C., which dealt with the State councils, gave our plans indorsement, together with full information and advice, and furnished letters of introduction. The officials of State councils in Virginia, Florida, Georgia, Alabama, and Kentucky extensively promoted the cooperative plan of organization. In Virginia, Kentucky, and Florida the executive secretary of the State Council of National Defense arranged for an appointment of white cooperating members of the Negro Workers' Advisory Committees. The Georgia council gave its advice to our State committee, the governor of Georgia, Hon. Hugh M. Dorsey, as chairman of the council, having issued the invitation for the State conference. The Alabama Council of National Defense appointed a Negro auxiliary to assist with the work. The Kentucky Council of National Defense was the main organization in promoting the formation of Negro Workers' Advisory Committees in its State.

The cooperation of private organizations and agencies, both local and national, was so hearty and widespread that it is practically impossible to name a list of the organizations that gave such cooperative service.

CHAPTER V.

NEGRO LABOR AND RACIAL RELATIONSHIPS AT CHICAGO.

[Extract from report of the Director of Negro Economics to the Secretary of Labor, through the Assistant Secretary on the subject of Negro labor situation in Chicago, Ill., and other localities, following race disturbances at Chicago.]

AUGUST 27, 1919.

Reports having been received at the office of the Secretary about disturbance at the stockyards in Chicago and other places of employment where Negroes have ordinarily been engaged, following the race riots in that city, after departmental conference, I was instructed by the Assistant Secretary to proceed to Chicago, St. Louis, Detroit, Cleveland, and near-by points in the territory to ascertain, first hand, the change, if any, in the labor situation. This report covers the results of a rapid survey of Chicago, of inquiries during a day at St. Louis, Mo., during brief visits to Detroit and Flint, Mich., and some statements secured on a stop-over in Cleveland on the return trip. I have also included the substance of reports from reliable Negroes, residents of several other cities.

THE CHICAGO SITUATION.

The disturbance in Chicago seems to have grown out of complex fundamental conditions, mainly economic. Some of the factors are not altogether labor factors but are largely the results of the labor and other economic conditions. From the testimony secured from localities other than Chicago, I am convinced, also, that the Chicago situation is partly typical, so far as the underlying factors in labor and other economic conditions are concerned.

Therefore, in giving full attention to it, we view conditions that are typical of many industrial centers. The demand for labor during the past five years drew large numbers of Negroes from the South. They have become almost putty in the hands of three more or less conflicting interests: (a) The employers, (b) white workmen, very largely organized, and (c) politicians.

1. Taking, first, the labor situation: In the early years of the stockyards development the labor supply was mainly American, German, and Irish that lived near the stockyards. When the stockyards were moved to their present location—at that time far removed from the residential and business districts of the city—Irish and German elements settled around the yards. With the coming of the Poles and other nationalities, following the great strike of 1904, the Irish were pushed across Halstead Street and beyond Thirty-ninth Street. The German element occupies neighborhoods on the other side of the yards and out toward Englewood.

With the growth of employment of Negroes in the stockyards, there has been continuous effort on the part of white workers to draw them into their unions. This has been only partially successful. Some dissatisfaction has resulted, and the union workers charged that the packers have used Negro leaders to prevent unionizing Negroes. The packers have denied any interference with the effort to unionize Negroes. It can not be told how much friction and feeling between the races this has caused. Testimony goes to show, however, that there has developed some friction between Negro workers and the Irish element at the yards. This did not seem to have any connection with the union situation but with individual contacts.

Whether this friction had any direct connection with the rioting is not fully established. All the testimony, however, shows that the point of greatest friction was where the Negro neighborhood touched the Irish neighborhood on the South Side. There was considerable mention in the testimony of an Irish athletic association, known as Regan's Colts. This was started as a sort of political and athletic association, but now has a reputation for considerable rowdyism.

2. The housing situation is another economic element. Many of those familiar with the conditions preceding the riots claim, however, that there is little relation between the feeling aroused about the housing and the riots. However that may be, it is certain that a large influx of Negroes (about doubling the Negro population of Chicago within five years) has created an acute housing situation on the South Side. This population has flowed out of the area previously occupied by Negroes and on into the areas occupied by whites, pressing upon the districts known as Englewood and Kenwood. The white residents have organized an association of residents. Reliable testimony, gained confidentially from some of their meetings, establishes the fact that there was considerable agitation, even suggestions of violence, to keep Negroes from renting and buying in the white district. Popular gossip connects the bombing of Negro residences with this agitation.

3. The political situation is a third factor of importance. These underlying forces of the attraction during the last five years of large numbers of Negro workers of the unskilled type, the friction over the housing congestion and the tension over political affairs were continually played upon and inflamed by agitation.

Some agitation arose from the persons highly active and prejudiced against Negroes. There were various clashes of individuals here and there. There were repeated attempts to frighten Negroes from residences by bombing their houses. There was quite a bit of newspaper publicity during the period of months preceding the riots.

All these incidents prepared the way for the underlying labor, housing, and political fires of friction to burst into the flames of riot and death. The occasion for the outbreak on Sunday, July 27, when white bathers stoned a Negro youth, knocking him from a raft and causing him to drown, was only the match which lighted the blaze.

4. The situation which developed at the stockyards, resulting in a walkout of many of the union employees, was only indirectly the result of the race riot. Some of the leaders of the Amalgamated Meat Cutters and Butcher Workmen of North America say that no strike was authorized, but that it is a code of the unions not to work in any place where police and military guards are over them.

Apparently the employers at the stockyards, fearing trouble when the Negroes returned to work on the Thursday following the riots, took the precaution of having extra police guards and details of militia. The union workmen interpreted the presence of these guardsmen as a move against them.   Immediately many of the union work-ers, among them some of the Negro union men, protested by leaving their work and by sending a committee of protest to public officials. Colored union men were on this committee.   By Monday of the following week, however, the militia had been removed and the resentment of the union men apparently quieted down.

Both the employees and the management of the stockyards testi-fied that there was no friction within the yards when the men re-turned to work.   Many evidences of good feeling and cooperation between white and colored workers were manifested.   The occasion was one, of course, when both the leaders of the unions and repre-sentatives of the packers were disclaiming any responsibility for the situation.

With this underlying condition confronting the community there was very limited contact between the more thoughtful and liberal-minded, social-minded citizens of the two races.   Barring the few leaders of the labor unions and a few representatives of philanthropic organizations there were few contacts through which there might be mutual understanding between the races.   The facts also seem to show that the large number of Negro unskilled workers directly from the South, both in their competition for work and in their needs for decent houses in good surroundings, were being used and ex-ploited.   The forces to help them, and thus to benefit the commu-nity, were few and comparatively weak.

It was also clear that the full sentiment of the employers, the largest of whom are the packers, favors the retention of the Negroes in Chicago.   On the other hand, the white union workers fear this competition of Negro workers unless they can induce them to enter the unions.

During the course of the riot the Association of Commerce called a conference of the representatives of 47 business and philanthropic organizations of the city at the Union League Club.   The outcome of this meeting was a resolution requesting the governor to appoint a committee "to study the psychological, sociological, and econom-ical causes underlying conditions resulting in the present race riot and to make such recommendation as will tend to prevent a recur-rence of such conditions in the future."

Gov. Lowden told me he had decided to appoint a local com-mission for Chicago only.   This will be composed of six white and six colored citizens of the highest standing   *   *   *.

5. From the nation-wide point of view another factor enters to make the Chicago situation complicated and of importance.   It is of special concern to this department in its relation to the whole matter of migration of Negro workers and the adjustment of their relations to white workers and white employers both north and south.

Immediately following the riots Chicago newspapers began to pub-lish dispatches, letters, and news items from southern territory invit-ing southern Negroes to return to the South for good treatment, peace, and employment.

During the week of my visit representatives of three different plant-ing interests of Mississippi were in the city, and it was reported that a delegation was on its way to Chicago from the Chamber of Com-merce in New Orleans with a colored man in the party to "pick the right type of Negroes."   *   *   *

It is uncertain just how far such an effort to induce Negroes to return to the South will be successful, but the effort has already aroused considerable opposition and discussion against it among Negroes, both in their newspapers and other channels. Of course immediately the ministers and newspapers are being accused of being paid by the packers, who want to hold the Negroes in Chicago. While there are no available facts to support such allegations, it is true that the employers of Chicago generally, according to testimony of the chairman of the Association of Commerce and other employers in touch with the situation, do not look with favor upon efforts made to take Negroes out of Chicago. * * *

The week of my visit, of course, was too soon to tell exactly how far the attitude of employers about employing Negroes had been affected by race riots. The examination of calls for Negro labor at two employment offices showed, however, that beginning with August 5, just after the close of the riots, there had been a gradual increase both in the number of calls for Negro help wanted, those referred, and those placed. Information could be secured for a few cases only where Negroes had been dropped during the days of the riots and had not been replaced when the situation quieted down. The facts so far obtainable indicate that in those employments where Negroes were used formerly there would probably not be any material change in the use of Negro workers.

Before summarizing the impressions gained in St. Louis, Mo., Detroit, Mich., and Cleveland, Ohio, it may be well to point out two other significant factors influencing the racial situation in Chicago as well as in other parts of the country. In the first place, there was a very widespread dissatisfaction, bordering on bitterness, among many Negroes, due to the reports they have received from the returning soldiers about their harsh treatment in the Army, both at home and in France. In many conversations and in public gatherings of Negroes some of these stories are rehearsed and commented upon. * * *

In the second place, there is a general feeling among all classes of Negroes that the Federal Government should do something to remedy their condition. This takes two forms: First, the abolition of evils. There is a very widespread and strong feeling that mobs and lynching and other abuses now affecting Negroes should be taken in hand by the Federal Government. Second, Negroes are looking to the Federal Government to take some constructive steps for their benefit. The great popularity of the action of the Department of Labor through the Division of Negro Economics for giving attention to working conditions of Negroes and their relation to white workers and white employers is largely due to this feeling of the Negroes that something should be done for them through the Federal Government. The Public Health Service of the Treasury Department is meeting with similar response. * * *

There is a frequent comment among Negroes on this point and questions are asked repeatedly why something in a large way is not done at this time. Larger efforts by Federal departments to improve living and working conditions among Negroes will receive hearty response from them.

In St. Louis a committee of colored citizens went to the chief of police during the days of the Washington-Chicago riots. They pledged him their support and made certain suggestions. He and the mayor immediately took steps to forestall any possible outbreaks. This, I was informed, led to special instructions to the patrolmen. Some newspaper publicity of a helpful kind was also obtained. Although several individual clashes were reported, the sentiment seems to be for quiet. It was reported, however, to me on good testimony that large numbers of Negroes have firearms and ammunition preparatory to protecting themselves and their homes in case of disturbances.

Detroit, Mich., has had a very large influx again during the past summer, the estimate being about 3,000 newcomers during the month of June alone. These newcomers comprise men, women, and children. While there is considerable congestion in one district there has, however, been considerable distribution of this Negro population in other sections of the city.

The race friction here has seemed to be small, probably due to the fact that the demand for labor is greater than the supply. Everybody is employed at high wages and so busy that there is hardly time for the frictions that go with unemployment. In some of the industrial plants employing large numbers of Negroes, the superintendents did take precaution during the days when the newspapers were reporting the riots in Washington and Chicago to prevent any possible friction between white and colored workers in their plants. For instance, one of the automobile accessories companies separated the white and colored workers in the lunch rooms as a precaution. The testimony indicates that this tended to cause friction rather than to prevent it, as it is reported that the colored workmen refused to share the lunch room with this new arrangement.

It was reported here also that Negroes have provided themselves with considerable firearms and ammunition lest trouble arise. One factor in the situation in Detroit making for harmony is the fact that the largest Negro neighborhood is bordered on one side by Jews, largely Russian, and on the other side by Italians. Cases of friction resulted only in individual clashes that had no group significance. During the days of the Washington-Chicago riots leading colored citizens conferred with the mayor and other officials about precautionary steps to prevent any possible outbreak.

In Cleveland, Ohio, there was some fear during the days of the riots elsewhere lest there might be some friction. An editorial in one of the colored newspapers, warning Negroes to arm themselves, drew forth an article from one of the white newspapers claiming that the chief of police had called this editor to task, threatening to arrest him for murder if any riot occurred and any one was killed. This was denied by the chief of police and the incident closed.

The colored editor, however, did receive some threatening letters and there was a report of an attack upon a Negro soldier by some white men in a high-powered automobile which ran into a Negro neighborhood. Both of these incidents caused some excitement among some of the colored people. There was, however, a feeling among some of the influential white and colored citizens that no race disturbance should take place in Cleveland.

Responsible citizens I interviewed, said however, that the city would welcome any cooperative effort to study the labor and other economic conditions looking toward measures that would prevent racial friction in the future.

From testimony of conditions which nearly resulted in riots in Sumter, S. C., Columbia, S. C., Birmingham, Ala., and from apprehension expressed and testimony as to preparations made by white and colored people in New York City, Jacksonville, Fla., and Montgomery, Ala., I am led to believe that the racial tension is so widespread as to be in fact a matter of national concern, calling for some attention from the National Government.

Respectfully submitted.

(Signed)   GEORGE E. HAYNES,
Director of Negro Economics.

CHAPTER VI.

WHITE AND NEGRO WORKERS IN BASIC INDUSTRIES.

The distribution of Negro workers in industries both as to States and the types of industries in which they were engaged in comparison with other workers in industries in the same States gives a good impression of their general part in war production and of the widespread contact of the racial labor relations. The facts are set forth in the tables of this chapter.

The first table (Table I) gives a general view of the white and Negro men engaged in industrial unskilled occupations in establishments in 1918 or at the height of our drive for war production. These figures were reported from the responsible employers themselves to the United States Employment Service when that service by Executive order took over the work of recruiting and placement of unskilled labor in all industries employing 100 or more men.

The data about establishments selected for this table were taken at random from the records of the hundreds that reported. The basis of selection was those employing 25 or more Negro workers. As many States as practicable were represented, so as to show the wide distribution of employment of Negroes, but those included are only a small part of the total number reporting. The estimate of the percentage of war work each establishment was doing, the number of hours per day, and the rate of wages are exactly as reported by each firm itself.

Unfortunately for the present purpose the reports did not show occupational distribution of these employees. The column showing the kind of industrial operation carried on by the firm could be classified only in the very general way here given, because of the brevity of description given in the reports. The classifications, however, give some general notion of the type of each plant or enterprise which was employing these men. A number of firms were omitted because the descriptions would not allow of even this general classification.

Table I, which follows below, shows enterprises in 26 States and the District of Columbia, which were, in 1918, employing 129,708 white men and 62,340 Negro men. Twelve Southern States and 14 Northern States are listed. If Ohio and Pennsylvania seem to have an undue number of firms listed in comparison with other States, especially in the South, it may be attributed to the large entrance of Negro migrants into their many industries, to the comparatively limited industrial development in the South, which is largely agricultural, and to the necessary exclusion of many firms in other States either because of their employment of less than 25 Negroes or because of insufficient information in their reports.

The percentage of war work upon which these enterprises were engaged shows the large part these men had in winning the war. Out of a total of 292 firms which gave information on this point only 23

32

reported less than 50 per cent war work and only 11 of these reported 25 per cent or less war work; 99 firms reported from 50 to 99 per cent war work and 151 firms reported 100 per cent war work. There might have been some bias in some cases, inasmuch as those firms having the greatest percentage of war work might have expected some priority in securing laborers.

The wage rates are also very interesting and indicate some contrasts for the same kind of industry in the different sections of the United States. For instance, unskilled workers in foundries were employed at the rate of $2.50 per 10-hour day in Alabama; from $3.50 per 10-hour day (one firm) to $4.25 per 9-hour day (one firm) in Illinois; $3.20 per 10-hour day (one plant, calculated from straight hourly rate) in Indiana; $2.50 per 10-hour day in Tennessee (only one firm) and $3.50 to $4 per 10-hour day (calculated from straight hourly rate) in Virginia.

Unskilled workers in iron and steel plants were employed at the rate of $2.50 to $3 per 10-hour day (one firm 9 to 12 hours with wages $2.25 to $3.79 per day, one firm 10 to 12 hours) in Alabama; from $3 to $4 per 10-hour day (calculated from straight hourly rate) in Illinois; from $2.75 to $3.60 (8, 9, 10, and 12 hour day differently in four plants) per day in Indiana; $3 per 10-hour day in Kentucky; from $2.88 to $4.95 per 9-hour day (calculated from straight hourly rate) in New York; from $3.40 to $4 per 10-hour day (calculated on straight hourly rate) in Ohio; from $3.20 to $6 (one plant reported 60 cents per hour) per 10-hour day (calculated from straight hourly rate) in Pennsylvania; from $2.40 to $3.20 per 8-hour day (calculated from the straight hourly rate) and $2.50 to $3 (one plant) per 10-hour day in Tennessee; and $2.75 per 12-hour day (one plant) in Virginia. It should be borne in mind constantly that during the stress of war production probably most plants ran longer than the regular hours and many of their employees worked overtime, the usual rule being to pay time and a half for overtime, and in some cases double time. Therefore no calculation of the actual average earnings of the workmen can be made from these rates of pay.

The full text of Table I with details by States follows, showing unskilled white and Negro male workers in selected typical war industries by States in 1918:

TABLE I.—*Unskilled white and Negro male workers in selected typical war industries employing 25 or more Negroes, with reported percentage of war work of each enterprise, hours, and wage rate, by States, 1918.*

ALABAMA.

Kind of industry of individual enterprise.	Number of unskilled workers. White.	Number of unskilled workers. Negro.	Percentage of war work in which workers were engaged at plant.	Number of hours in working day.	Rate of wages. Per hour.	Rate of wages. Per day.
1	2	3	4	5	6	7
Ammunition	46	58	5	10		$2.50–3.50
Army ordnance	45	200	100	10	$0.30	
Cement	102	88	100	12		2.50–3.00
Chemicals	41	122	100	9	.31	
Coal and iron	14	84	100	10	0.30–.33	
Fertilizer	3	25	(1)	10		2.50–3.00
Foundry	50	75	100	10		2.50
Do	22	178	95	10		2.50
Do	(1)	110	100	9	.25	
Do	26	317	100	10		2.50
Iron and steel	(1)	25	100	10		3.00
Do	25	75	100	10		3.00
Do	6	136	25	10		2.50–2.75
Do	16	171	93	9–12		2.25–3.25
Do	350	600	95	10–12		2.25–3.79
Lumber	100	100	75	10		2.25–2.50
Sawmill	5	60	100	10		2.00–2.50
Do	16	37	100	10		2.50
Shipbuilding	150	100	100	8	.30–.40	
Do	5	189	98	8	.40	
Do	750	500	90	8	.30–.40	
Steel wire	9	211	30	10	.30	
Railroad	20	300	100	10	.34	
Do	73	1,420	100	10	.34	
Radiators	1	25	75	9	.35	

CONNECTICUT.

Kind of industry of individual enterprise.	White.	Negro.	Percentage of war work.	Hours.	Per hour.	Per day.
Ammunition	200	50	100	10		$3.50–3.90
Iron	400	100	100	10	$0.40	
Metal	1,800	45	90	(1)	.33	
Shells	219	59	100	11	.40	

DELAWARE.

Kind of industry of individual enterprise.	White.	Negro.	Percentage of war work.	Hours.	Per hour.	Per day.
Powder	45	30	100	8	$0.40	
Do	60	44	100	10	.40	
Pyrites	29	67	100	10	.40	
Shells	120	80	100	10	.40	
Steel castings	28	27	100	9	0.37–.40	
War supplies	89	95	90	9¾	.36	

DISTRICT OF COLUMBIA.

Kind of industry of individual enterprise.	White.	Negro.	Percentage of war work.	Hours.	Per hour.	Per day.
Electric equipment	30	51	100	10	$0.40	
Paper	30	52	50	8	.35	

FLORIDA.

Kind of industry of individual enterprise.	White.	Negro.	Percentage of war work.	Hours.	Per hour.	Per day.
Lumber	232	217	100	10	$0.25	
Do	50	225	100	10		$2.00
Do	20	465	100	10		1.80–2.25
Do	150	350	90	11		2.00–2.50
Naval stores	11	324	80	10		2.40

[1] No figures available.

TABLE I.—*Unskilled white and Negro male workers in selected typical war industries employing 25 or more Negroes, with reported percentage of war work of each enterprise, hours, and wage rate, by States, 1918*—Continued.

GEORGIA.

Kind of industry of individual enterprise.	Number of unskilled workers. White.	Number of unskilled workers. Negro.	Percentage of war work in which workers were engaged at plant.	Number of hours in working day.	Rate of wages. Per hour.	Rate of wages. Per day.
1	2	3	4	5	6	7
Cotton	134	169	12	10	$0.30	....
Iron	(1)	147	80	10	....	$2.00
Lumber	75	225	100	10	....	2.00
Turpentine	(1)	300	80	8	0.25-.35	....

ILLINOIS.

Kind of industry of individual enterprise.	White.	Negro.	Percentage	Number of hours.	Per hour.	Per day.
Aluminum	1,000	500	90	8	....	$3.10
Canning	2,921	410	80	10	$0.40	....
Castings	1,450	225	70	10	.36	....
Cork	1,658	281	35	9	.35	....
Foundry	300	75	95	10	....	3.50
Do	268	162	77	9	....	3.50-4.25
Iron	350	150	40	10	.40	....
Lumber	175	126	75	10	....	2.25-2.75
Meat	4,110	3,244	21	8	.40	....
Meat packing	3,714	2,375	80	8	.40	....
Paint	1,300	50	80	10	0.35-.40	....
Shells	836	417	100	10	....	3.50
Steel	250	250	100	10	.30-.38	....
Stockyards	1,151	604	25	8	.40	....
Do	3,250	1,087	75	8	.40	....
Zinc	350	50	100	8	....	3.00-3.90

INDIANA.

Kind of industry of individual enterprise.	White.	Negro.	Percentage	Number of hours.	Per hour.	Per day.
Foundry	75	150	70	10	$0.32	....
Gas	470	156	100	8	.35	....
Iron	(1)	34	90	10	....	$2.75-3.00
Do	81	112	95	9	.35	....
Do	30	120	100	12	....	3.60
Iron and steel	154	98	75	8	.30	....
Picric acid	50	50	100	10	.40	....
Plates	1,350	500	100	10	.42	....
Steel	550	50	(1)	10	.33	....

IOWA.

Kind of industry of individual enterprise.	White.	Negro.	Percentage	Number of hours.	Per hour.	Per day.
Building	152	101	47	9	....	$4.05
Foodstuffs	800	25	30	8	$0.37-.40	....
Meat	860	101	85	8	.40	....

KANSAS.

Kind of industry of individual enterprise.	White.	Negro.	Percentage	Number of hours.	Per hour.	Per day.
Meat packing	375	75	90	8	$0.37	....
Do	2,062	746	40	10	.40	....
Mining	125	25	50	(1)	.41	....

[1] No figures available.

TABLE I.—*Unskilled white and Negro male workers in selected typical war industries employing 25 or more Negroes, with reported percentage of war work of each enterprise, hours, and wage rate, by States, 1918*—Continued.

KENTUCKY.

Kind of industry of individual enterprise.	Number of unskilled workers.		Percentage of war work in which workers were engaged at plant.	Number of hours in working day.	Rate of wages.	
	White.	Negro.			Per hour.	Per day.
1	2	3	4	5	6	7
Boilers	137	55	(1)	10	$0.27-.40	
Boxes	438	75	(1)	10		$1.75
Iron	140	153	100	9¾		3.00
Do	994	225	40	10	.30	
Leather	10	50	100	9½	.30	
Lumber	10	73	(1)	9½		2.50
Signal corps	27	56	100	11		

LOUISIANA.

Kind of industry of individual enterprise.	White.	Negro.			Per hour.	Per day.
Lumber	45	175	100	10		$2.75-3.00
Do	1,000	2,000	100	10		2.00-2.50
Shipbuilding	50	150	100	9	$0.30	
Do	90	304	100	10	.30-.40	

MARYLAND.

Kind of industry of individual enterprise.	White.	Negro.			Per hour.	Per day.
Ammunition	703	600	100	8		$3.00
Copper	2,300	200	100	8		3.20

MASSACHUSETTS.

Kind of industry of individual enterprise.	White.	Negro.			Per hour.	Per day.
Electrical work	1,200	50	100	9	$0.28-.30	
Steel castings	150	50	100	9	.37½	
Sugar	410	90	100	9	.37	

MISSISSIPPI.

Kind of industry of individual enterprise.	White.	Negro.			Per hour.	Per day.
Sawmill	1	125	(1)	10		$1.50-2.50
Do	38	310	100	10		1.75
Wood products	100	900	100	10		2.75-3.25

NEBRASKA.

Kind of industry of individual enterprise.	White.	Negro.			Per hour.	Per day.
Meat	140	45	(1)	8	$0.40	
Metal	400	100	100	8		$3.20

NEW JERSEY.

Kind of industry of individual enterprise.	White.	Negro.			Per hour.	Per day.
Shells	244	200	100	8	$0.35	
Tubes	50	40	100	(1)	.22-.40	
Shrapnel loading	350	325	100	9	.40	

1No figures available.

TABLE I.—*Unskilled white and Negro male workers in selected typical war industries employing 25 or more Negroes, with reported percentage of war work of each enterprise, hours, and wage rate, by States, 1918*—Continued.

NEW YORK.

Kind of industry of individual enterprise.	Number of unskilled workers.		Percentage of war work in which workers were engaged at plant.	Number of hours in working day.	Rate of wages.	
	White.	Negro.			Per hour.	Per day.
1	2	3	4	5	6	6
Aluminum	750	50	100	8–10	$0.34–.40	
Do	2,700	400	100	8		$3.50
Chemicals	1,000	75	100	9		3.25
Elevators	470	30	90	8	.35	
Glass	500	40	100	10		
Machinery	851	98	100	10	.35	
Valves	146	32	98	9	.36	
Steel	550	50	100	9	.32–.55	
Do	395	98	80	9	.37–.40	
Sugar	600	57	100	10	.35–.38	

NORTH CAROLINA.

Kind of industry of individual enterprise.	White.	Negro.	Percentage.	Hours.	Per hour.	Per day.
Aluminum	704	792	100	8		$2.50
Cotton towels	14	65	48	10	$0.15	
Lumber	15	200	80	11		2.00–2.75
Do	20	280	(¹)	10		1.00–2.50
Do	25	300	80	10		2.25–3.00
Shipbuilding	200	50	100	10	46	
Sewerage	(¹)	180	100	10		2.75

OHIO.

Kind of industry of individual enterprise.	White.	Negro.	Percentage.	Hours.	Per hour.	Per day.
Aluminum	125	220	90	9	$0.38	
Automobiles	4,500	300	15	9	035–.37½	
Bottles	350	50	40	8–10		$2.75–3.50
Bronze	30	30	70	8–9	.40–.45	
Castings	80	46	95	9–12		3.25–3.75
Chain	103	82	100	10	.30	
Do	143	142	100	10		3.00
Chemicals	3	50	100	10	.35	
Fertilizer	55	55	100	10		3.50–3.85
Foundry	425	175	85	10		3.75
Do	225	150	85	10	.40	
Fuses	200	100	98	10	.35	
Guns	580	525	100	11	.32½	
Heaters	24	117	40	10	.35–.45	
Ink	240	25	40	8¾		3.50–3.85
Rolling mill	58	62	100	10	.34	
Shells	27	26	75	10	.37½	
Steel	1,300	400	90	10	.38–.40	

OKLAHOMA.

Kind of industry of individual enterprise.	White.	Negro.	Percentage.	Hours.	Per hour.	Per day.
Meat packing	843	376	80	8	$0.37	
Petroleum	77	35	100	9		$3.00

¹ No figures available.

TABLE I.—*Unskilled white and Negro male workers in selected typical war industries employing 25 or more Negroes, with reported percentage of war work of each enterprise, hours, and wage rate, by States, 1918*—Continued.

PENNSYLVANIA.

Kind of industry of individual enterprise.	Number of unskilled workers. White.	Number of unskilled workers. Negro.	Percentage of war work in which workers were engaged at plant.	Number of hours in working day.	Rate of wages. Per hour.	Rate of wages. Per day.
1	2	3	4	5	6	6
Acids	100	45	100	9	$0.40	
Aero engines	346	110	95	9½	.42	
Air brakes	722	67	95	9½	.42	
Aluminum	1,300	100	90	9–10	.34–.41	
Ammunition	1,500	300	100	10		$4.07
Benzol	25	33	100	10	.37½	
Boilers	1,071	120	100	14	.38	
Bolts	80	30	95	10	.37½	
Do	350	100	(1)	10		3.50
Do	485	35	94	10½	.34½	
Boxes	262	29	65	10	.35–.45	
Bricks	50	60	100	10		3.00
Do	195	35	100	10–12		3.15–5.52
Bronze	50	20	95	10	.32½	
Building	14	86	70	11–15	.40	
Cars	475	25	100	10	.34–.39	
Castings	15	75	95	9¾	.38–.45	
Do	70	45	100	9		3.15
Do	200	100	100	10		3.50–3.60
Do	250	80	99	9–10	.38–.41	
Do	307	120	98	10	.38–.45	
Cement	430	40	95	10		3.80–6.00
Chemicals	60	40	100	10	.40	
Do	119	95	100	9½		3.89–4.81
Do	150	100	100	10–12	.41–.46	
Coal	113	159	100	10	.32	
Coal tar	150	75	80	10		3.80
Do	240	33	(1)	9–10	.40	
Construction	10	50	10			4.00
Cork	120	27	100	10	.35	
Dredges	175	25	95	10		3.00–3.50
Electric supplies	503	152	71	10		3.50–4.20
Electric work	150	57	50	9		3.60
Engines	100	25	75	9¾	.32	
Explosives	1,701	175	100	8	.40	
Fertilizer	235	109	(1)	10	.38	
Gasoline	1,413	359	100	9	.40	
Gas engines	910	29	97	10		3.30–3.85
Glass	250	50	50	9		3.50
Do	589	280	10	8		2.96
Gypsum	3	68	70	10		4.00–4.50
Houses	50	200	100	10		4.40
Iron	90	30	100	12	.41	
Do	93	92	90	10	.38	
Do	100	25	100	10	.40	
Do	425	25	100	11	.37½	
Do	600	150	70	10	.35	
Do	729	258	90	10	.38	
Iron and steel	2,200	1,808	100	10	.32	
Iron bars	75	35	80	8–10	.35–.45	
Do	190	55	68	3 24		3.84
Leather	21	54	100	9	.35–.45	
Do	74	36	60	9		2.88
Do	53	106	90	10		4 16.20
Lime	180	60	100	10	.28–.30	
Lumber	40	90	85	10	.35	
Machines	65	75	100	(1)	.35	
Magnesia	55	30	90	10¾	2 .29	
Do	120	70	85	10¼	.35	
Metal	62	40	100	10		4.20
Molding	468	32	92	12	.28	
Munitions	2,600	1,900	90	9½	.39	
Nuts	80	40	79	10½	.28–.35	
Oils	6,000	250	100	10	.40–.45	
Optical glass	50	85	75	8		2.80–3.60

1 No figures available.   2 Plus bonus.   3 Probably more than one shift.   4 Week.

TABLE I.—*Unskilled white and Negro male workers in selected typical war industries employing 25 or more Negroes, with reported percentage of war work of each enterprise, hours, and wage rate, by States, 1918*—Continued.

PENNSYLVANIA—Continued.

Kind of industry of individual enterprise.	Number of unskilled workers.		Percentage of war work in which workers were engaged at plant.	Number of hours in working day.	Rate of wages.	
	White.	Negro.			Per hour	Per day.
1	2	3	4	5	6	6
Ordnance	3,000	1,000	100	10–12	$0.33–.50	
Pig iron	29	25	100	10–11		$3.97–4.20
Do	• 85	40	100	10		4.55
Do	300	200	100	10–12		3.15
Do	1,000	600	60	10–12	.38	
Pipe fittings	200	30	95	10	.33	
Plate glass	150	30	33½	10–11		3.25
Powder	1,008	65	100	8	.38–.45	
Railroad cars	84	86	100	10	.37½	
Plate tin	349	61	100	11½	.38	
Refrigerators	497	56	100	10	.30–.32	
Rifles	500	1,500	100	10	.35–.37½	
Rivets and nails	107	58	95	10½	.35	
Shells	50	50	100	10	.42	
Do	200	90	100	10	.37½	
Do	950	40	97	10	.35	
Sheet copper	150	60	100	9		3.45
Shipbuilding	319	78	100	10		3.50
Soap	171	81	(¹)	8		2.80
Steel	7	26	100	12	.30	
Do	35	30	100	10		3.45–3.90
Do	35	30	100	10	.60	
Do	50	50	100	10	.40	
Do	76	114	100	8		4.50
Do	100	30	95	10		4.00
Do	130	75	100	10	.35–.48	
Do	150	50	100	10		4.40
Do	334	32	85	10½	.38	
Do	340	40	80	10	.38	
Do	470	425	100	10¼	.40	
Do	500	150	98	12	.38	
Do	940	77	100	12		4.14
Do	701	344	100	10	.38	
Do	1,242	543	90	9		3.45
Do	3,000	400	100	10	.38	
Steel castings	8	32	100	9½	.34–.40	
Do	70	45	100	9		3.15
Steel goods	350	31	75	10½	.38	
Steel hooks	600	165	100	11½	.38	
Steel plates	257	296	100	10		3.20–3.84
Do	7,750	850	87	10	.35	
Sugar	710	220	100	8–10		3.28–3.80
Tires	725	20	100	10		3.50
Tools	500	25	100	11½		4.37
Warehouses	400	325	100	8	.35	
Wire	650	25	75	10	.38	

RHODE ISLAND.

Linters	92	196	100	8	$0.32	

SOUTH CAROLINA.

Lumber	55	190	3	10		$2.00–2.50
Do	10	125	45	10	$0.25–.30	
Do	29	218	100	10		

¹ No figures available.

TABLE I.—*Unskilled white and Negro male workers in selected typical war industries employing 25 or more Negroes, with reported percentage of war work of each enterprise, hours, and wage rate, by States, 1918*—Continued.

TENNESSEE.

Kind of industry of individual enterprise.	Number of unskilled workers.		Percentage of war work in which workers were engaged at plant.	Number of hours in working day.	Rate of wages.	
	White.	Negro.			Per hour.	Per day.
1	2	3	4	5	6	6
Aluminum	287	263	100	10	....	$2.25–2.50
Boxes	187	188	75	11	....	[1] 1.75
Brake shoes	4	154	100	10	....	2.40–3.00
Cement	154	120	100	10	$0.25	....
Chemicals	10	100	100	10	([2])	([2])
Foundry	130	120	100	10	....	2.50
Iron	375	100	85	8	.30–.38	....
Do	525	375	100	10	....	2.50–3.00
Do	900	600	98	8	.30–.40	....
Planing mill	143	69	95	10	....	2.50
Shells	550	250	100	8	.30–.40	....

TEXAS.

Bridges	300	30	100	10	$0.30–.40	....
Iron	6	45	100	9	.30–.33½	....
Lumber	75	70	100	10	....	$2.50–6.00
Do	40	120	100	10	....	2.75
Shipbuilding	40	80	100	11	.30	....

VIRGINIA.

Ammunition boxes	25	125	100	10	....	$3.85
Cement	100	50	70	10	....	3.50–5.00
Chains	1	40	100	10	$0.35	....
Chemicals	250	75	100	9	.35	....
Do	....	30	....	10	....	4.00
Commissary contractor	150	150	100	8	....	2.50
Creosoted material	10	65	90	10	.35–.40	....
Fertilizer	16	53	....	10	.38½	....
Do	30	30	....	10	....	4.00
Foundry	5	58	100	10	.35–.40	3.75
Do	12	54	90	10	.35	....
Guncotton	1,158	5,233	100	8	.35–.44	....
Houses	80	204	100	11	.35–.40	....
Land and gravel	10	40	100	11	....	3.00
Lime	57	35	95	10	....	2.50
Lumber	116	49	78	10	....	3.25–4.25
Do	200	75	75	9	....	3.00–4.00
Do	([2])	30	50	9	....	3.00
Paving	([2])	250	100	10	....	3.85
Pig iron	5	85	100	12	....	2.75
Pipe	70	75	70	10	....	2.00–5.00
Shell loading	870	1,336	100	8	....	3.84
Tobacco	475	275	25	10	.35	....

[1] With board.   [2] No figures available.

To ascertain more definitely and more in detail facts needed in understanding the problems involved in the Negro's new relation to industry, the Inspection and Investigation Service undertook an intensive study of several basic industries employing Negroes in 1918–19. Mr. Byron K. Armstrong and two other investigators were sent to visit establishments that were employing perhaps large numbers of Negroes. The study had to be discontinued before completion because the service under which it was being made was abolished after failure of appropriations. The data, therefore, cover only a few plants in Illinois, Ohio, and Pennsylvania and does not include other States as originally planned. The conclusions that might have been drawn, therefore, will necessarily be deferred until further data is available.

The facts and figures that were secured, however, are illuminating and instructive. The table which follows below (Table II) gives the details as to kinds of occupations, the average number of hours worked per week, the average earnings per week, and the average earnings per hour of 4,260 white men and 2,722 Negro men in 194 occupations in 23 establishments, for six basic industries—foundries, slaughtering and meat packing, automobiles, coke ovens, iron and steel and their products, and glass manufacturing. A supplement to this table (Table II) gives similar figures for 153 white and 83 Negro women in slaughtering and meat packing.

The occupations shown in these two tables have been classified as skilled, semiskilled, and unskilled. This classification, to be sure, is uncertain and open to serious question but is the best designation feasible under our present lack of occupational analysis.

The Bureau of Labor Statistics, Department of Labor, says in its introductory statement to the first report on its "Description of Occupations":

These descriptions of occupations are based on investigations, including private interviews and correspondence, extending over practically the entire United States. The one outstanding fact coming from this investigation is that there are no standards or generally accepted occupational names or definitions.

The classification in the tables given below, however, were made as carefully as possible, with the assistance of the employment experts of the plants visited, upon the basis of descriptions of the actual processes the worker performed. They are not presented as conclusive, but only as indicative of the standards in proficiency required and pay received for such work. Some occupations, "carpenters" for instance, have been classed as unskilled or semiskilled that on further consideration might be otherwise listed. This has been done in line with the classification of work into grades and placing the work done in a particular establishment in the class that seems most indicative of its grade.

Two comparisons from Table II—the average hourly earnings of Negro workers and the average number of hours worked per week— call for comment. There were 85 occupations in which 5 or more Negro men and 5 or more white men each were engaged in the 23 plants. Of these occupations 8 were classified as skilled, 25 were classified as semiskilled, and 52 were classified as unskilled.

For purposes of these comparisons on the average hours worked per week and average hourly earnings some cases of the same occupations in which five or more Negro workers and five or more white workers were employed in different plants were reckoned as a different unit of comparison of hours and of wages. The average number of hours worked per week and the average weekly earnings are based upon figures taken from the official records of each establishment.

The foundries were the only plants that employed any considerable number of Negroes in skilled occupations. In 6 foundries there were 6 units of comparison in skilled occupations on the basis here described; meat packing and slaughtering establishments reported only 1 such unit of comparison in skilled occupations; 5 automobile establishments reported no skilled occupations in which 5 or more Negroes were employed; coke ovens (1 establishment) and glass manufacturing (1 establishment) had no skilled occupations in which 5 or more Negroes were employed and only 1 out of 8 iron and steel plants reported 1 skilled occupation which had a basis for such unit of comparison.

The fact that foundries have such a large representation of Negroes in skilled occupations may be explained partly because Negroes have probably had longer industrial experience in this industry than the other occupations listed, except possibly coke ovens. In the table, only 1 coke oven establishment is included, so a comparison can not be made. In the South, for more than a generation foundries have employed Negroes as molders and in other skilled and semiskilled work. When Negro workers migrated North, this was the line in which many of them had good skill and long experience. Their non-appearance in skilled occupations in iron and steel plants may be partly because their entrance in large numbers into these plants was to replace immigrant and foreign-born laborers who were doing mainly semiskilled and unskilled work, partly because of the small proportion of skilled work in the industry, partly because some organized crafts in the industry were opposed to the employment of Negroes in their trade, and partly because not a great many Negroes possessed necessary training and experience to qualify for skilled work in this field.

Taking such comparisons of skilled units in the foundries which were studied, Negro workers showed a higher average number of hours worked per week than white workers in 3 units and a higher average earnings per hour in 1 unit. In 3 units Negro workers showed a lower average number of hours worked per week than white workers and in 5 units a lower average of earnings per hour than white workers.

In the one unit of comparison of skilled occupations in slaughtering and meat-packing establishments Negro workers showed a higher average number of hours worked per week and a higher average of earnings per hour than white workers. In the one unit of comparison of skilled occupations in the iron and steel industry the Negro workers showed a lower average number of hours worked per week and lower average earnings per hour than white workers.

Turning to units of comparison for occupations classed as semiskilled, in 5 foundries Negro workers showed a higher average number of hours worked per week than white workers in 3 units and a higher average earnings per hour in 3 units. Negro workers made a lower average number of hours worked than white workers in 2 units and a lower average earnings per hour in 2 units. In slaughtering and meat packing, in 1 unit of comparison of semiskilled occupations, Negro workers made a higher average number of hours worked and a higher average earnings per hour than white workers.

In automobile establishments in 6 units of comparison of semiskilled occupations, Negro workers showed the same average number of hours worked as white workmen and the same average earnings per hour. , In the coke ovens establishment, Negro workers showed a higher average number of hours than white workers in 1 unit and a higher average earnings per hour in 1 unit; a lower average number of hours worked than white workers in 1 unit and a lower average earnings per hour in 2 units. In iron and steel plants Negro workers showed a higher average number of hours worked than white workers in 3 units of semiskilled occupations and a higher average earnings per hour in 2 units; a lower average number of hours than white workers in 1 unit and a lower average earnings per hour in 1 unit. Negro workers showed the same average number of hours worked per week as white workers in 6 units and the same average earnings per week in 7 units. In glass manufacture Negro workers showed a lower average number of hours worked in 1 unit of semiskilled occupations and a lower average hourly earnings in 1 unit.

Taking the semiskilled group as a whole for all establishments employing 5 or more Negro workers and 5 or more white workers, there are 25 units of comparison. These show that Negro workers had a higher average number of hours worked per week than white workers in 8 units and a higher average earnings per hour in 8 units, about one-third in each. Negro workers showed a lower average number of hours worked per week than white workers in 5 units and a lower average earnings per hour in 5 units, about one-fourth in each. Negro workers showed the same average number of hours worked per week as white workers in 12 units and the same average earnings per hour in 12 units.

The occupations classed as unskilled furnish the largest number of units of comparison—52 in all. In the foundries Negro workers showed a higher average number of hours worked per week than white workers in six units and a higher average earnings per hour in five units. They showed a lower average number of hours worked per week than white workers in two units, a lower average earnings per hour in four units, and the same average number of hours worked per week as white workers in one unit. In slaughtering and meat packing Negro workers made a higher average number of hours worked per week than white workers in four units of unskilled occupations and a higher average earnings per hour in two units. They showed a lower average number of hours worked than white workers in four units and lower average earnings per hour in six units.

In automobile establishments Negro workers showed the same average number of hours worked as white workers and the same average earnings per week in seven units of unskilled occupations. At the coke ovens plant Negro workers showed a higher average number of hours worked per week than white workers in seven units and a higher average earnings per hour in five units. They showed a lower average number of hours worked per week than white workers in four units and lower average earnings per hour than white workers in six units.

In the iron and steel industries Negro workers made a higher average number of hours worked per week than white workers in four units and a higher average earnings per hour in six units of unskilled occupations. They showed a lower average number of hours worked per week than white workers in six units and lower average earnings per week than white workers in four units. They showed the same average number of hours worked per week as white workers in five units and the same average earnings per week as white workers in five units. In the glass manufacturing establishment Negro workers showed a higher average number of hours worked per week than white workers and a lower average earnings per week than white workers in two units of comparison of unskilled occupations.

Taking the 52 units of comparison of unskilled occupations as a whole, Negro workers showed a higher average number of hours worked per week than white workers in 23 units, nearly one-half of the total, and a higher average earnings per week in 18 units, a little more than one-third of the total number. They showed a lower average number of hours worked per week than white workers in 16 units, or a little less than one-third of the total number, and a lower average earnings per hour in 22 units or about two-fifths of the total number. Negro workers showed the same average number of hours worked per week as white workers in 13 units, or about one-fourth of the total number, and the same average earnings per week week as white workers in 12 units of unskilled occupations, or less than one-fourth of the total number.

To sum up the comparison of unskilled units, Negro workers showed a higher average number of hours than white workers in nearly one-half of the total number of units of comparison, a lower average number of hours worked per week in a little less than one-third of the total number, and the same average number of hours worked per week in about one-fourth of the total number of units. The Negro workers showed a higher average earnings per week than white workers in a little more than one-third of the total number of units; a lower average weekly earnings in about two-fifths of the total number of units, and the same average earnings per week as white workers in less than one-fourth of the total number of units of white and Negro workers compared in unskilled occupations.

Taking the total 85 units of comparison for the three classifications of skilled, semiskilled, and unskilled occupations in all the establishments, the Negro workers showed a higher average number of hours worked per week than white workers in 35 units, or considerably more than one-third of the total number of units; a lower average number of hours worked per week in 25 units, or less than one-third, and the same average number of hours worked per week as white workers in 25 units, or less than one-third of the total units of comparison.

Negro workers showed higher average earnings per hour than white workers in 28 units, or about one-third of the total number of units of comparison in the three classes of occupations; they showed lower average earnings per week in 33 units, or considerably more than one-third of the total; and the same average earnings per week in 24 units, or somewhat less than one-third of the total number of units of comparison in all the occupations listed.

The figures in detail of Table II, showing classification of occupations, the number of white and Negro employees, and the average number of hours of work per week and the average earnings per week and per hour of white and Negro workers in the specified occupations follows:

TABLE II.—*Comparative table of "average hours of work" and "average earnings" of male white and Negro employees engaged in specified occupations of six basic industries—1918–19.*

[S, skilled; S–S, semiskilled; Un–S, unskilled.]

Establishment No.	Occupation.	Kind of occupation.	Number of employees.		Average number of hours worked per week.		Average earnings per week.		Average earnings per hour.	
			White.	Negro.	White.	Negro.	White.	Negro.	White.	Negro.
	FOUNDRY (IRON AND STEEL).									
1	Carpenters............	S–S...	1	1	59.00	38.00	$23.60	$15.20	$0.4000	$0.4000
	Furnace men........	S–S...	1	11	67.75	62.00	28.79	26.47	.4249	.4269
	Grinders.............	S–S...	16	7	40.65	45.40	15.49	17.71	.3811	.3900
	Laborers.............	Un–S.	78	233	48.55	46.95	17.41	19.08	.3585	.4063
	Millwrights..........	S......	1	1	58.75	58.25	26.44	24.76	.4500	.4250
	Molders.............	S–S...	12	11	52.75	48.15	30.22	24.88	.5728	.5167
2	Core makers........	S......	7	1	54.30	56.00	28.44	30.38	.5237	.5425
	Chippers............	S–S...	10	1	43.30	53.00	22.98	25.18	.5307	.4751
	Electric welders.....	S......	3	1	57.30	57.00	38.63	39.90	.6742	.7000
	Grinders............	S–S...	2	5	48.50	44.90	27.39	24.08	.5647	.5363
	Laborers............	Un–S.	29	59	58.30	58.70	24.70	24.54	.4237	.4181
3	.....do.............	Un–S.	42	35	68.20	68.65	23.96	23.56	.3513	.3432
	Molders.............	S......	140	38	51.50	47.20	25.23	22.09	.4899	.4680
	Core makers........	S......	24	24	47.70	55.60	31.12	29.24	.6524	.5259
	Molders[1]...........	S......	29	24	49.20	53.30	28.53	30.99	.5799	.5814
	.....do.[1]..........	S......	16	8	50.80	50.85	28.71	27.78	.5652	.5463
5	Laborers............	Un–S.	62	69	48.40	43.30	24.91	21.79	.5147	.5032
	Molders.............	S......	33	35	47.90	45.40	28.47	24.35	.5944	.5363
5A	Carpenters..........	S–S...	45	2	50.40	48.10	26.29	23.71	.5216	.4929
	Casting chippers....	S–S...	5	4	38.10	48.40	14.97	19.10	.3929	.3946
	Casting cleaners.....	Un–S.	5	32	40.30	50.60	15.21	20.82	.3774	.4115
	Core-room helpers...	S–S...	6	6	35.30	40.00	12.05	14.87	.3414	.3717
	Craters.............	S–S...	26	1	42.50	28.50	17.56	9.23	.4132	.3239
	Cupola helpers......	S–S...	1	7	35.20	52.90	13.83	22.77	.3929	.4304
	Floor molders.......	S......	24	11	40.80	37.60	25.38	21.54	.6221	.5729
	Foundry helpers....	S–S...	12	17	31.00	41.90	11.78	15.76	.3800	.3761
	Helpers.............	Un–S.	6	6	42.70	52.20	17.27	20.43	.4044	.3914
	Janitors............	Un–S.	3	5	50.00	44.80	18.24	15.33	.3648	.3422
	Laborers............	Un–S.	40	19	43.00	43.00	17.74	18.75	.4126	.4360
	Oven tenders........	S–S...	2	2	43.10	51.50	20.39	20.07	.4731	.3897
	Sweepers............	Un–S.	26	10	45.50	55.90	14.50	19.02	.3187	.3403
	Yardmen............	Un–S.	2	1	51.00	51.00	16.95	12.67	.3324	.2484
5B	Chippers............	S–S...	17	3	[2]60.25	[2]65.00	[2]31.85	[2]47.50	.5287	.7308
	Cub molders........	S–S...	1	8	58.50	56.80	27.19	28.34	.4648	.4990
	Cupola men.........	S–S...	2	4	65.00	62.60	31.00	27.71	.4769	.4427
	Japanners..........	S–S...	3	1	[2]58.50	[2]58.50	[2]32.74	[2]32.85	.5597	.5615
	Laborers............	Un–S.	37	7	[2]56.30	[2]63.05	[2]23.18	[2]25.98	.4117	.4121
	Molders.............	S......	54	3	[2]50.50	[2]39.65	[2]35.89	[2]29.19	.7107	.7362
	Molders' apprentices.	Un–S.	2	6	[2]62.50	[2]55.40	[2]25.00	[2]26.88	.4000	.4851
	Molders' helpers....	S–S...	16	13	[2]64.80	[2]54.25	[2]29.12	[2]26.31	.4494	.4850
	Shake-out men......	S–S...	1	6	[2]37.50	[2]33.35	[2]37.21	[2]34.63	.9922	1.0383
	SLAUGHTERING AND MEAT PACKING.									
6	Backers.............	S......	4	2	68.20	71.50	49.44	51.84	.7249	.7264
	Brinze trimmers.....	S......	3	1	67.50	67.50	30.04	30.04	.4450	.4450
	Caul pullers.........	S......	2	1	64.50	54.80	31.92	27.10	.4949	.4945
	Droppers (hoist)....	Un–S.	1	6	67.50	65.50	29.03	28.18	.4301	.4302
	Fell beaters........	S......	1	1	74.00	74.00	32.93	32.93	.4450	.4450
	Gutters.............	S......	1	3	67.50	67.70	33.75	33.88	.5000	.5004
	Headers...........•..	S......	3	1	51.20	59.80	29.17	34.06	.5697	.5696
	Knockers............	S......	1	2	68.50	68.50	32.54	31.85	.4750	.4650
	Laborers............	Un–S.	18	27	68.90	70.60	27.57	28.24	.4001	.4000
	Leg breakers........	S......	2	5	67.50	62.90	32.07	29.88	.4751	.4827
	Pritchers-up........	Un–S.	1	1	64.00	67.50	27.52	29.03	4300	.4301
	Rumpers............	S......	4	1	67.90	69.80	45.18	35.93	.6654	.5148
	Rump sawyers......	S......	1	1	67.50	68.00	33.75	34.00	.5000	.5000
	Splitters............	S......	5	1	67.50	67.50	53.67	53.67	.7951	.7951
	Switchers-on rail....	Un–S.	5	2	79.50	69.00	34.19	30.95	.4301	.4485
	Truckers............	S–S...	2	14	55.50	63.90	23.87	27.48	.4301	.4300
	Beef casings:									
	Gut runners.....	S......	2	1	70.90	67.50	36.85	35.10	.5197	.5200
	Laborers........	Un–S.	3	11	64.20	71.50	25.68	28.59	.4000	.3999
	Machinemen....	S–S...	5	1	74.60	67.50	32.08	29.03	.4300	.4301
	Strippers........	S......	1	3	67.50	69.50	30.72	31.63	.4551	.4551

[1] Different types of molders.   [2] Compiled on a piecework basis.

Table II.—*Comparative table of "average hours of work" and "average earnings" of male white and Negro employees engaged in specified occupations of six basic industries—1918-19—Continued.*

[S, skilled; S-S, semiskilled; Un-S, unskilled.]

Establishment No.	Occupation.	Kind of occupation.	Number of employees.		Average number of hours worked per week.		Average earnings per week.		Average earnings per hour.	
			White.	Negro.	White.	Negro.	White.	Negro.	White.	Negro.
	SLAUGHTERING AND MEAT PACKING—con.									
6	Dry salt:									
	Dippers	S–S	1	1	66.50	46.30	$28.60	$19.88	$0.4301	$0.4294
	Graders	S–S	2	1	76.90	51.30	33.05	22.02	.4298	.4292
	Nailers	Un–S	5	1	56.30	67.00	23.37	28.81	.4151	.4300
	Packers	Un–S	3	2	52.20	58.30	22.70	25.05	.4349	.4297
	Pilers	Un–S	5	5	62.90	63.90	27.02	27.09	.4296	.4239
	Rubbers	Un–S	5	5	64.70	59.90	26.85	24.83	.4150	.4145
	Truckers	Un–S	12	12	65.50	61.30	26.20	24.53	.4000	.4002
	Hog heads:									
	Laborers	Un–S	3	4	57.20	68.00	22.87	27.20	.3998	.4000
	Skin heads	S	1	1	61.10	61.10	27.20	27.20	.4452	.4452
	Hog killing:									
	Laborers	Un–S	24	32	72.30	62.30	28.94	24.92	.4003	.4000
	Shave sides	S	1	2	57.40	57.40	26.10	26.10	.4547	.4547
	Snatchers	S	1	1	97.00	97.00	44.59	44.72	.4597	.4610
	Sausage-making:									
	Laborers	Un–S	36	2	47.80	69.20	19.12	27.67	.4000	.3999
7	Beef killing:									
	Backers	S	2	2	66.00	66.00	52.20	52.20	.7909	.7909
	Fell beaters	S	2	2	66.00	66.00	31.68	31.68	.4800	.4800
	Fell cutters	S	2	1	59.80	66.00	33.60	37.08	.5619	.5618
	Foot skinners	S	3	2	62.30	43.00	30.26	20.68	.4857	.4809
	Gullet raisers	S–S	1	2	53.50	65.80	24.54	31.18	.4587	.4739
	Gutters	S	2	2	66.00	64.50	36.00	35.00	.5455	.5426
	Headers	S	1	6	65.00	64.20	40.18	39.76	.6181	.6193
	Knockers	S	2	2	66.00	66.00	33.48	33.48	.5073	.5073
	Laborers	Un–S	20	18	56.20	54.80	24.43	23.83	.4347	.4349
	Leg breakers	S	4	6	46.40	62.50	24.10	32.48	.5194	.5197
	Rump sawyers	S	3	3	47.30	65.80	25.75	35.89	.5444	.5454
	Splitters	S	1	3	66.00	66.00	57.24	57.24	.8673	.8673
	Repair department:									
	Steamfitters	S	52	13	65.70	72.60	37.68	41.76	.5735	.5752
8	Canning department (bacon):									
	Butchers	S–S	3	11	57.70	56.90	25.89	25.83	.4487	.4540
	Laborers	Un–S	100	84	58.40	59.10	25.21	25.45	.4317	.4306
	Nailers	S–S	41	2	56.30	51.50	24.85	22.80	.4414	.4427
9	Beef coolers:									
	Knifemen	S–S	14	13	64.80	67.80	27.33	29.11	.4218	.4294
	Laborers	Un–S	20	34	58.70	59.90	23.41	23.88	.3988	.3987
	Pieceworkers	S	3	4	61.30	47.90	48.00	30.83	.7830	.6436
	AUTOMOBILES.									
10	Boiler room	S–S	6	4	50.00	50.00	22.57	22.57	.4514	.4514
	Connecting rod department.	S–S	25	1	50.00	50.00	30.00	22.80	.6000	.4560
	Enamel rubbers	S–S	16	4	50.00	50.00	35.75	24.75	.7150	.4950
	Lathe department	S–S	60	1	50.00	50.00	30.00	30.00	.6000	.6000
	Machine shop	S–S	8	1	50.00	50.00	30.00	30.00	.6000	.6000
	Motor assembling	S–S	30	1	50.00	50.00	38.75	38.75	.7750	.7750
	Piston department	S–S	30	1	50.00	50.00	30.00	30.00	.6000	.6000
	Sand-blast room	Un–S	9	2	50.00	50.00	33.00	33.00	.6600	.6600
	Stock tracers	Un–S	15	4	50.00	50.00	20.79	20.79	.4158	.4158
11	Core makers	S	6	2	55.00	55.00	33.55	33.55	.6100	.6100
	…..do	S–S	25	25	55.00	55.00	28.60	28.60	.5200	.5200
	Heaters	S–S	22	45	55.00	55.00	26.40	26.40	.4800	.4800
	Inside laborers	Un–S	128	136	55.00	55.00	24.20	24.20	.4400	.4400
	Janitors	Un–S	20	109	55.00	55.00	23.10	23.10	.4200	.4200
	Stock handlers	Un–S	73	14	55.00	55.00	26.40	26.40	.4800	.4800
	Truck drivers	S–S	19	3	55.00	55.00	26.40	26.40	.4800	.4800
	Truckers	S–S	24	134	55.00	55.00	23.10	23.10	.4200	.4200
12	Chippers	Un–S	8	12	55.00	55.00	26.40	26.40	.4800	.4800
	Machine molders	S–S	54	15	55.00	55.00	33.00	33.00	.6000	.6000
	Grinders	Un–S	10	4	55.00	55.00	26.40	26.40	.4800	.4800
	Mold rammers	S–S	25	25	55.00	55.00	33.00	33.00	.6000	.6000
	Molders	S	6	3	55.00	55.00	44.00	44.00	.8000	.8000
13	Janitors	Un–S	10	20	50.00	50.00	22.50	22.50	.4500	.4500
	Laborers	Un–S	80	40	50.00	50.00	22.50	22.50	.4500	.4500
	Sweepers	Un–S	50	65	50.00	50.00	22.50	22.50	.4500	.4500
	Truckers	S–S	100	60	50.00	50.00	22.50	22.50	.4500	.4500

TABLE II.—*Comparative table of "average hours of work" and "average earnings" of male white and Negro employees engaged in specified occupations of six basic industries—1918–19*—Continued.

[S, skilled; S–S, semiskilled; Un–S, unskilled.]

Establishment No.	Occupation.	Kind of occupation.	Number of employees.		Average number of hours worked per week.		Average earnings per week.		Average earnings per hour.	
			White.	Negro.	White.	Negro.	White.	Negro.	White.	Negro.
	COKE OVENS.[3]									
14	Battery-door hoisters	S–S...	10	6	[3] 144.90	[3] 131.30	[3]$71.12	[3]$64.17	$0.4908	$0.4887
	Battery-house laborers.	Un–S.	11	6	[3] 161.70	[3] 150.00	[3] 77.25	[3] 70.76	.4777	.4717
	Battery laborers.....	Un–S.	11	17	[3] 150.30	[3] 156.50	[3] 68.88	[3] 73.04	.4582	.4668
	By-product labor....	Un–S.	15	26	[3] 139.60	[3] 149.50	[3] 65.73	[3] 70.70	.4708	.4729
	Coal unloaders......	Un–S.	46	16	[3] 163.20	[3] 163.80	[3] 80.32	[3] 75.58	.4922	.4614
	Coke loaders........	Un–S.	9	1	[3] 142.60	[3] 167.50	[3] 68.62	[3] 85.52	.4812	.5106
	Crane engineers.....	S......	3	2	[3] 156.00	[3] 155.00	[3] 96.30	[3] 92.75	.6173	.5984
	Door cleaners.......	Un–S.	6	1	[3] 165.90	[3] 143.00	[3] 78.38	[3] 67.72	.4638	.4736
	Dryermen..........	Un–S.	20	6	[3] 151.70	[3] 161.70	[3] 73.01	[3] 77.03	.4813	.4764
	Firemen............	Un–S.	1	25	[3] 180.00	[3] 152.70	[3] 87.50	[3] 74.24	.4861	.4862
	Foremen............	S......	2	1	[3] 156.00	[3] 168.00	[3] 98.58	[3] 104.43	.6319	.6216
	Gas tenders.........	Un–S.	5	13	[3] 158.10	[3] 153.20	[3] 80.10	[3] 77.41	.5066	.5053
	Laborers...........	Un–S.	149	36	[3] 149.80	[3] 143.00	[3] 76.55	[3] 79.08	.5110	.5530
	Larrymen...........	S–S...	5	15	[3] 108.50	[3] 155.20	[3] 53.17	[3] 76.08	.4900	.4902
	Lidsmen............	Un–S.	5	20	[3] 160.70	[3] 156.20	[3] 77.36	[3] 75.07	.4814	.4806
	Luttermen..........	Un–S.	31	13	[3] 152.20	[3] 157.60	[3] 73.44	[3] 75.90	.4825	.4816
	Patchers...........	Un–S.	12	1	[3] 148.00	[3] 144.00	[3] 69.81	[3] 68.04	.4717	.4725
	Pencilmen..........	Un–S.	30	9	[3] 142.50	[3] 154.90	[3] 66.35	[3] 72.92	.4656	.4708
	Pushers............	S–S...	12	1	[3] 158.30	[3] 167.50	[3] 77.70	[3] 82.16	.4908	.4905
	Salt wheelers.......	Un–S.	6	2	[3] 133.30	[3] 134.00	[3] 63.29	[3] 72.18	.4748	.5387
	Standpipe men......	Un–S.	5	16	[3] 160.70	[3] 144.60	[3] 77.21	[3] 69.92	.4807	.4835
	Sulphate laborers...	Un–S.	30	3	[3] 140.90	[3] 164.00	[3] 66.30	[3] 77.24	.4736	.4710
	Water tenders.......	S–S...	3	1	[3] 175.00	[3] 180.00	[3] 94.27	[3] 97.12	.5387	.5396
	IRON AND STEEL AND THEIR PRODUCTS.									
	Transportation:									
	Switchmen.....	S.....	45	12	74.35	72.40	41.56	40.47	.5590	.5589
	Plate mill:									
	Cindersnappers.	Un–S.	3	1	78.00	60.00	39.06	30.04	.5007	.5057
	Hookers........	Un–S.	2	1	66.00	68.00	31.44	32.16	.4764	.4726
	Laborers.......	Un–S.	17	1	67.85	70.00	31.51	30.13	.4644	.4304
	Pushers........	Un–S.	5	5	73.40	75.80	51.72	51.68	.7046	.6811
	Scrapmen.......	Un–S.	12	15	74.20	74.45	51.99	51.33	.7007	.6894
	Shear helpers...	Un–S.	22	23	77.55	71.05	52.00	50.47	.6705	.7103
	Blast furnace:									
	Cinder laborers..	Un–S.	36	3	72.35	64.00	35.52	31.42	.4909	.4909
	First helpers....	S–S...	21	18	69.75	61.90	34.14	30.31	.4895	.4896
	Handymen......	Un–S.	1	6	78.00	73.80	45.05	42.25	.5775	.5725
	Keepers, furnace	S......	18	4	73.75	75.00	40.73	41.20	.5523	.5493
	Laborers........	Un–S.	121	20	64.50	62.65	30.04	29.43	.4657	.4697
	Larrycar helper.	Un–S.	35	6	73.10	62.00	35.75	30.41	.4890	.4905
	Larrycar operators.	S–S...	22	2	62.60	63.00	34.78	33.08	.5555	.5250
	Stockhouse laborers.	Un–S.	3	6	54.00	48.85	25.91	22.85	.4798	.4678
15	Gas makers.....	S–S...	1	10	67.00	69.70	24.74	25.59	.3693	.3671
	Laborers........	Un–S.	4	2	44.60	46.50	18.18	16.38	.4076	.3523
16	Do.........	Un–S.	212	146	81.55	69.55	33.99	35.57	.4168	.5114
	Do.........	S–S...	53	10	85.85	91.70	43.51	45.29	.5068	.4939
17	Car checkers....	Un–S.	2	1	62.25	50.00	29.13	19.95	.4680	.3990
	Furnacemen....	Un–S.	8	11	67.70	62.75	33.86	31.60	.5001	.5036
	Inspectors......	S–S...	15	2	61.40	61.40	30.71	32.69	.5002	.5324
	Laborers........	Un–S.	12	13	60.95	61.50	25.62	26.83	.4203	.4363
	Machine operators.	S–S...	21	3	55.65	48.40	35.35	25.40	.6352	.5248
	Spring formers..	S–S...	21	4	63.05	37.55	54.19	33.00	.8595	.8788
18	Assemblers......	S–S...	74	1	50.00	50.00	22.50	22.50	.4500	.4500
	Laborers........	Un–S.	19	20	50.00	50.00	20.00	20.00	.4000	.4000
	Machine hands..	S.....	145	1	50.00	50.00	35.00	35.00	.7000	.7000
	Maintenance....	S–S...	55	20	50.00	50.00	22.50	22.50	.4500	.4500
	Picklers and sharers.	S–S...	16	13	50.00	50.00	22.50	22.50	.4500	.4500
	Piercers.........	S–S...	95	24	50.00	50.00	22.50	22.50	.4500	.4500

[3] Average number of hours and average earnings under this coke-oven schedule were available only for a period of 13 days, and it was impracticable, therefore, to try to estimate the weekly hours and earnings.

TABLE II.—*Comparative table of "average hours of work" and "average earnings" of male white and Negro employees engaged in specified occupations of six basic industries—1918-19—Continued.*

[S, skilled; S–S, semiskilled; Un–S, unskilled.]

Estab-lish-ment No.	Occupation.	Kind of occu-pation.	Number of em-ployees.		Average num-ber of hours worked per week.		Average earn-ings per week.		Average earn-ings per hour.	
			White.	Negro.	White.	Negro.	White.	Negro.	White.	Negro.
	IRON AND STEEL AND THEIR PRODUCTS—continued.									
	Blast furnace—Con.									
18	Punch press hands.	S–S...	16	1	50.00	50.00	$22.50	$22.50	$0.4500	$0.4500
	Punch press helpers.	Un–S .	46	17	50.00	50.00	20.00	20.00	.4000	.4000
	Stock handlers..	Un–S .	13	8	50.00	50.00	20.00	20.00	.4000	.4000
19	Hammermen's helpers.	S–S...	113	14	41.05	41.15	21.35	21.72	.5201	.5278
	Laborers (raw material).	Un–S .	57	23	52.60	49.25	21.33	19.93	.4055	.4047
20	Sweepers........	Un–S .	2	7	47.00	53.60	15.82	16.84	.3367	.3142
	Truckers........	S–S...	5	18	49.25	50.00	15.95	17.08	.3238	.3416
21	Yardmen........	Un–S .	6	47	55.30	62.45	17.98	19.39	.3251	.3105
	Nutmakers.....	S–S...	3	2	53.50	53.50	25.47	25.47	.4750	.4750
	Do..........	Un–S .	1	1	53.50	48.50	24.08	18.68	.4500	.3852
	Packing.........	S–S...	7	2	53.50	53.50	24.08	24.08	.4500	.4500
22	Trimmers.......	S–S...	8	1	53.50	35.00	19.32	20.63	.3611	.5894
	Coring..........	S–S...	29	6	53.00	53.00	22.79	22.79	.4300	.4300
	Forcing.........	Un–S .	47	28	53.00	53.00	22.79	22.79	.4300	.4300
	Furnace........	S–S...	77	13	53.00	53.00	22.79	22.79	.4300	.4300
	Molding.........	S–S...	15	18	53.00	53.00	22.79	22.79	.4300	.4300
	Stock room.....	Un–S .	28	7	53.00	53.00	22.79	22.79	.4300	.4300
	MANUFACTURING GLASS.									
23	Keepers..........	Un–S .	30	16	48.80	49.60	14.75	14.09	.3023	.2841
	Packers..........	S–S...	27	11	53.20	50.70	16.72	15.08	.3143	.2974
	Producermen.......	S–S...	10	2	56.70	60.60	22.65	21.00	.3995	.3465
	Yard laborers........	Un–S .	36	6	60.10	69.40	18.52	20.21	.3082	.2912

Comparative table of "average hours of work" and "average earnings" of female white and Negro employees engaged in specified occupations in the slaughtering and meat-packing industry.

Occupation.	Kind of occu-pation.	Number of employees.		Average number of hours worked per week.[1]		Average earnings per week.		Average earnings per hour.		Total "regu-lar" hours per week.	
		White.	Negro.	White.	Negro.	White.	Negro.	White.	Negro.	White.	Negro.
HOG-HEAD PREPA-RATION.											
Washers and trim-mers.	Un–S.	7	7	57.4	57.4	$19.50	$19.50	$0.3397	$0.3397	48	48
SAUSAGE MANUFAC-TURING.											
Casings workers....	Un–S.	9	12	48.8	49.1	15.09	14.96	.3092	.3047	48	48
Sausage-tying workers.	Un–S.	6	1	47.8	46.6	14.48	14.22	.3029	.3052	48	48
Stuffing-room workers.	Un–S.	20	13	50.5	46.7	16.87	16.04	.3341	.3436	48	48
CANNING DEPART-MENT (BACON).											
Bacon wipers.......	Un–S.	2	8	56.0	55.1	17.69	17.41	.3159	.3160	48	48
Can oilers..........	Un–S.	9	2	57.1	59.5	18.11	18.87	.3172	.3171	48	48
Can painters........	Un–S.	9	2	52.3	36.0	34.11	22.36	.6522	.6211	48	48
Can wipers.........	Un–S.	36	19	53.0	57.3	16.78	18.16	.3166	.3169	48	48
Scalers.............	Un–S.	22	4	55.2	51.5	19.41	17.65	.3516	.3427	48	48
Solder droppers.....	Un–S.	6	3	50.6	56.2	16.09	17.80	.3180	.3167	48	48
Wrappers...........	Un–S.	27	12	51.2	56.5	16.20	17.86	.3164	.3161	48	48

[1] The number of hours in excess of 48 should be regarded as "overtime."

TABLE III.—*Opinions of 38 employers of Negro workers showing the attitude of firms toward Negro labor, the opportunities for promotion, and opinion on comparative behavior of white and colored employees for 101,458 white and 6,757 colored employees,[1] 1918–19.*

	To what extent are Negroes admitted to skilled occupations?	Does the management recruit Negro skilled workmen locally or from distant points?	Does the management promote Negro workmen to the skilled ranks?	Is there equal opportunity for unskilled Negro workmen to learn semiskilled or skilled processes as white workmen?	Do the Negro workmen show ambition for advancement?	Is there any difference in the conduct and behavior of Negro and white workers in the plant?	What difference, if any, in the loss of materials due to defective workmanship between white and Negro employees?	What time is required to break in employees to the work and what difference, if any, exists between white and Negro workers?	Is there a Negro labor adviser? If so, what are the results of his advice?	Number of persons on the pay roll.		
										Total.	White.	Negro.
1	Full opportunity	Locally	Yes	Yes	No	Yes[2]	None	Equal time	No	118	51	67
2	Extent of ability[3]	...do	Yes	Yes	Yes, small number	No record	No comparison	No record	Yes, 3; no record	506	239	267
3	Small extent	No record	No record	Yes	Yes	No	No record	Two weeks, equal	No	45	2	43
4	Same as whites	Locally	Yes	Yes	No	No	No difference	No difference	No	16	2	14
5	...do	...do	Yes	Yes	Yes	No	None	One week, equal	No	23	10	13
6	Full extent[4]	...do	Yes	Yes	Not as a whole	No	No record	Varies, equal time	Yes[5]	591	526	65
7	Same basis as white	...do	Yes	Yes	Yes[6]	No[7]	None	No difference	No	6,200	6,000	200
8	Skilled women, 135	...do	Yes, women	Yes	Yes	Yes[7]	...do	Longer for colored	No	6,200	6,000	200
9	To all except office work	...do	Yes	Yes	Yes	Yes	...do	No difference	No	84	42	42
10	Small extent	...do	Yes	Yes	Yes	No	No difference	About the same	No			
11	To all occupations	No recruiting	Yes	Yes	Yes	No	No record	No record				
12	To the majority	Locally	Yes	Yes[8]	Yes, a few	None	...do	...do	Yes; no record	1,589	1,364	225
13	Extent of ability	...do	Yes	Yes	Yes[9]	Yes[10]	None	Two weeks, equal	No	1,326	1,320	6
14	According to ability	...do	Yes	Yes	Yes, a few	No	...do	No record	No	3,157	3,145	12
15	On the same basis	...do	Yes	Yes	Yes	No	...do	...do	No	449	358	91
16	All branches	...do	Yes	Yes	Not as a rule	No	...do	...do	No	4,826	4,553	273
17	None	...do[11]	Yes	Yes	Yes	No	...do	No difference	No	8,396	7,719	677
18	...do	...do[11]	No discrimination	Yes	Not in all cases	No	...do	Less time for whites	No	6,500	6,400	100
19	According to ability	...do	Yes	Yes	Not as a rule	No	...do	No difference	No	42,892	41,963	929

#											
20	Butchers, only	..do..	Yes[12]	..do..	Yes[13]	No record	Same time	No	99	38	61
21	Same as whites	do	Yes	Not generally	Yes[14]	No difference	No record	No	3,200	1,920	1,280
22	No discrimination	do	Yes	do	No	None	do	No	700	593	107
23	do	do	Yes	do	No	do	No difference	No	807	740	67
24	Not at all	do	Yes, semiskilled	In some cases	No	do	No difference	No	560	518	42
25	No skilled Negroes	do[15]	Yes	Yes	No	No record	No record	No	394	361	33
26	No discrimination	do	Yes	No	No	None	do	No	51	34	17
27		do	Yes, when efficient		Yes[16]	No difference	Longer for colored				
28	Same as any other class	do	Yes[17]	Yes		None	Equal time		6,346	5,231	1,115
29	Molders, only	do	No[17]		No	do	Depends upon person	No			
30	Not as mechanics[18]	do	Yes	Same as whites	No	No difference	About the same	No	84	42	42
31	All except pattern making	do	Yes[19]	Yes	No	None	No difference	No	24	16	8
32	Only to molders	do	Yes, molders	Yes	No	The same	About the same	No	107	70	37
33	According to ability	None employed	Yes	In rare cases	Yes	None	The same	No	7,850	7,510	340
34	Small extent only		No	No	Yes[20]		Longer for Negroes	No	277	201	76
35	None in skilled lines	Locally	Yes	Not as a rule	No	Greater for colored		No	1,364	1,243	121
36	No limits	do	Yes	Some do	No	About the same	Same time, both	No	191	164	27
37	Semiskilled, only	do	Yes, semiskilled	Same as whites	No	do	do	No	117	23	94
38	None	None employed	No	Not as a rule	No	do	No record	No	3,126	3,060	66
	Total								108,215	101,458	6,757

1 Approximate number.
2 Negroes are more inclined to loaf.
3 Except as to molders.
4 Except three trades, as to which the union members make objection.
5 Not known as such to the workers.
6 But not as much as might be wished for.
7 Negroes are late oftener and have poorer attendance records.
8 From the standpoint of the company, not from the standpoint of the workmen.
9 To a marked degree.
10 Negro workers "visit," quite a deal of the time.
11 Locally for ordinary labor; Negro skilled workmen not employed.
12 Butchers and meat curers.
13 Negro workers not as serious as white workers.
14 Conduct and behavior of Negro workers caused by high turnover.
15 Ordinary workmen,
16 Not as steady as whites.
17 Excepting molders and carpenters.
18 Because of labor troubles.
19 Excepting pattern making.
20 Negro men will not work steadily.

CHAPTER VII.

STATISTICS ON THE MEAT-PACKING AND STEEL INDUSTRIES.

One of the evidences of the growing importance of Negroes in northern industries is shown by the increasing percentage of Negroes employed in one or two of the large meat-packing establishments in Chicago during 1916, 1917, and 1918, and a steel.company of Indiana Harbor for all the months of 1918.

In the first meat-packing company, beginning July 13, 1918, and running through to February 28, 1919, it is shown that at the beginning of this period there were 4,734 white employees, or 81.89 per cent, and 1,047 Negro employees, or 18.11 per cent of the labor force. There were 796 white women, or 87.19 per cent, and 117 Negro women, or 12.81 per cent. At the close of the period there were 4,925 white employees, or 83.38 per cent, and 982 Negro employees, or 16.62 per cent of the total number, while there were 821 white women constituting 89.24 per cent, and 99 Negro women, or 10.76 per cent of the total number of employees. These figures indicate the importance in numbers and percentage of Negro workers in the slaughtering and meat-packing industry, for the total number of white employees at the beginning of the period was 81.89 per cent and at the close 83.38 per cent and the number of Negro employees at the beginning of the period was 18.11 per cent and at the close 16.62 per cent. This shows that there was a slight reduction in the percentage of Negro employees, both male and female, during the period, but that the reduction was very light, being slightly more than 1.5 per cent for Negro men and 2 per cent for Negro women.

The table following shows the details of the variation by weeks:

52

TABLE IV.—*Number of employees of the first meat-packing company, distributed by color and sex, for a period of 30 successive weeks, beginning July 13, 1918.*

Week No.	Total number of employees, white and colored, male and female.	Total number of employees, distributed by color				Male employees					Female employees				
		White.	Per cent.	Colored.	Per cent.	Total.	White.	Per cent.	Colored.	Per cent.	Total.	White.	Per cent.	Colored.	Per cent.
1	5,781	4,734	81.89	1,047	18.11	4,868	3,938	80.90	930	19.10	913	796	87.19	117	12.81
2	5,792	4,714	81.39	1,078	18.61	4,916	3,953	80.41	963	19.59	876	761	86.87	115	13.13
3	5,802	4,762	82.07	1,040	17.93	4,832	3,906	80.84	926	19.16	970	856	88.25	114	11.75
4	5,840	4,716	80.75	1,124	19.25	4,853	3,883	80.01	970	19.99	987	833	84.40	154	15.60
5	5,995	4,887	81.52	1,108	18.48	4,912	3,969	80.80	943	19.20	1,083	918	84.76	165	15.24
6	5,937	4,860	81.86	1,077	18.14	4,883	3,962	81.14	921	18.86	1,054	898	85.20	156	14.80
7	6,036	4,883	80.89	1,153	19.11	4,874	3,922	80.47	952	19.53	1,162	961	82.70	201	17.30
8	5,981	4,873	81.47	1,108	18.53	4,907	3,968	80.86	939	19.14	1,074	905	84.26	169	15.74
9	5,916	4,810	81.30	1,106	18.70	4,820	3,893	80.77	927	19.23	1,096	917	83.67	179	16.33
10	5,919	4,864	82.18	1,055	17.82	4,800	3,920	81.67	880	18.33	1,119	944	84.36	175	15.64
11	5,826	4,824	82.80	1,002	17.20	4,765	3,924	82.35	841	17.65	1,061	900	84.83	161	15.17
12	5,852	4,826	82.47	1,026	17.53	4,743	3,956	81.68	887	18.32	1,009	870	86.22	139	13.78
13	5,844	4,865	83.25	979	16.75	4,780	3,921	82.03	859	17.97	1,064	944	88.72	120	11.28
14	5,753	4,775	83.00	978	17.00	4,721	3,868	81.93	853	18.07	1,032	907	87.89	125	12.11
15	5,445	4,490	82.46	955	17.54	4,471	3,650	81.64	821	18.36	974	840	86.24	134	13.76
16	5,570	4,623	83.00	947	17.00	4,548	3,725	81.90	823	18.10	1,022	898	87.87	124	12.13
17	5,787	4,779	82.58	1,008	17.42	4,680	3,818	81.58	862	18.42	1,107	961	86.81	146	13.19
18	5,803	4,771	82.22	1,032	17.78	4,735	3,855	81.41	880	18.59	1,068	916	85.77	152	14.23
19	5,785	4,744	82.01	1,041	17.99	4,729	3,834	81.07	895	18.93	1,056	910	86.17	146	13.83
20	6,115	4,994	81.67	1,121	18.33	4,950	3,970	80.20	980	19.80	1,165	1,024	87.90	141	12.10
21	6,045	4,916	81.32	1,129	18.68	4,977	3,981	79.99	996	20.01	1,068	935	87.55	133	12.45
22	6,319	5,134	81.25	1,185	18.75	5,283	4,232	80.11	1,051	19.89	1,036	902	87.07	134	12.93
23	6,360	5,166	81.23	1,194	18.77	5,343	4,281	80.12	1,062	19.88	1,017	885	87.02	132	12.98
24	6,565	5,369	81.78	1,196	18.22	5,499	4,440	80.74	1,059	19.26	1,066	929	87.15	137	12.85
25	6,346	5,231	82.43	1,115	17.57	5,315	4,334	81.54	981	18.46	1,031	897	87.00	134	13.00
26	6,380	5,239	82.12	1,141	17.88	5,355	4,349	81.21	1,006	18.79	1,025	890	86.83	135	13.17
27	6,362	5,284	83.06	1,078	16.94	5,374	4,420	82.25	954	17.75	988	864	87.45	124	12.55
28	6,372	5,311	83.35	1,061	16.65	5,409	4,463	82.51	946	17.49	963	848	88.06	115	11.94
29	6,180	5,052	81.75	1,128	18.25	5,153	4,215	81.80	938	18.20	1,027	837	81.50	190	18.50
30	5,907	4,925	83.38	982	16.62	4,987	4,104	82.29	883	17.71	920	821	89.24	99	10.76

The figures of the second meat-packing company give a very large showing of the increasing use of Negro employees in this plant, one of the largest in the industry. At the beginning of the period (January, 1916, to January, 1919, or a period of 159 weeks), the plant was employing a total of 8,361 employees. Of these, 8,050, or 96.28 per cent, were white and 311, or 3.72 per cent, were colored. The full figures cover the period just preceding the entrance of the United States into the war, the entire period during which our country was at war, and approximately the three months following the signing of the armistice. The total number of employees of this firm gradually increased until it reached the mark of 16,989 employees during the last week in November, 1918, and 17,434 during the third week of December, 1918. The number of colored employees, however, increased more rapidly in proportion than the number of white employees, reaching a maximum of 24.09 per cent of the total in March, 1918, and ranging from that time on between 17 and 21 per cent of the total. At the close of the period, February, 1919, the firm was employing 13,928 workers, of whom 11,123, or 79.86 per cent, were white employees and 2,805, or 20.14 per cent, were colored employees. This shows a proportionate increase, nearly fivefold, in the number of Negro employees.

TABLE V.—*Number of employees of the second meat-packing company, distributed by color, for a period of 159 successive weeks, January, 1916, to January, 1919. (See graphs following.)*

Week No.	Total number of employees, white and Negro, male and female.	Total number of employees, distributed by color.				Week No.	Total number of employees, white and Negro, male and female.	Total number of employees, distributed by color.			
		White.	Per cent.	Negro.	Per cent.			White.	Per cent.	Negro.	Per cent.
1	8,361	8,050	96.28	311	3.72	37	9,316	8,007	85.95	1,309	14.05
2	7,989	7,683	96.17	306	3.83	38	9,180	7,927	86.35	1,253	13.65
3	8,008	7,699	96.14	309	3.86	39	9,425	8,101	85.95	1,324	14.05
4	7,941	7,569	95.32	372	4.68	40	9,620	8,240	85.65	1,380	14.35
5	7,824	7,470	95.48	354	4.52	41	9,872	8,344	84.52	1,528	15.48
6	7,904	7,527	95.23	377	4.77	42	10,084	8,637	85.65	1,447	14.35
7	7,889	7,476	94.76	413	5.24	43	10,129	8,673	85.63	1,456	14.37
8	8,084	7,673	94.92	411	5.08	44	10,229	8,686	84.92	1,543	15.08
9	8,037	7,637	95.02	400	4.98	45	10,394	8,830	84.95	1,564	15.05
10	8,213	7,824	95.26	389	4.74	46	10,630	8,977	84.45	1,653	15.55
11	8,330	7,938	95.29	392	4.71	47	10,749	9,057	84.26	1,692	15.74
12	8,141	7,795	95.75	346	4.25	48	10,980	9,070	82.60	1,910	17.40
13	8,123	7,766	95.61	357	4.39	49	10,582	8,802	83.18	1,780	16.82
14	7,971	7,632	95.75	339	4.25	50	10,135	8,450	83.37	1,685	16.63
15	7,982	7,591	95.10	391	4.90	51	10,284	8,579	83.42	1,705	16.58
16	7,766	7,363	94.81	403	5.19	52	10,173	8,495	83.51	1,678	16.49
17	7,414	6,941	93.62	473	6.38	53	10,255	8,598	83.84	1,657	16.16
18	7,158	6,604	92.26	554	7.74	54	10,428	8,700	83.43	1,728	16.57
19	7,479	6,947	92.89	532	7.11	55	10,473	8,746	83.51	1,727	16.49
20	7,449	6,935	93.10	514	6.90	56	10,188	8,614	84.55	1,574	15.45
21	7,399	6,900	93.26	499	6.74	57	10,175	8,525	83.78	1,650	16.22
22	7,421	6,907	93.07	514	6.93	58	10,075	8,423	83.60	1,652	16.40
23	7,705	7,121	92.42	584	7.58	59	10,102	8,469	83.83	1,633	16.17
24	7,696	7,101	92.27	595	7.73	60	10,155	8,503	83.73	1,652	16.27
25	7,811	7,184	91.97	627	8.03	61	10,145	8,510	83.88	1,635	16.12
26	7,937	7,270	91.60	667	8.40	62	10,036	8,372	83.41	1,664	16.59
27	8,062	7,329	90.91	733	9.09	63	10,142	8,464	83.45	1,678	16.55
28	8,306	7,532	90.68	774	9.32	64	10,223	8,512	83.26	1,711	16.74
29	8,081	7,309	90.45	772	9.55	65	10,115	8,243	81.49	1,872	18.51
30	8,123	7,312	90.02	811	9.98	66	10,264	8,384	81.68	1,880	18.32
31	8,514	7,495	88.03	1,019	11.97	67	10,533	8,673	82.34	1,860	17.66
32	8,681	7,657	88.20	1,024	11.80	68	10,646	8,697	81.69	1,949	18.31
33	8,884	7,831	88.15	1,053	11.85	69	10,640	8,722	81.97	1,918	18.03
34	8,959	7,837	87.48	1,122	12.52	70	10,416	8,442	81.05	1,974	18.95
35	8,737	7,654	87.60	1,083	12.40	71	10,452	8,504	81.36	1,948	18.64
36	9,134	7,830	85.72	1,304	14.28	72	10,181	8,199	80.53	1,982	19.47

TABLE V.—*Number of employees of the second meat-packing company, distributed by color, for a period of 159 successive weeks, January, 1916, to January, 1919. (See graphs following)*—Continued.

Week No.	Total number of employees, white and Negro, male and female.	Total number of employes, distributed by color.				Week No.	Total number of employees, white and Negro, male and female.	Total number of employees, distributed by color.			
		White.	Per cent.	Negro.	Per cent.			White.	Per cent.	Negro.	Per cent.
73	10,385	8,312	80.04	2,073	19.96	117	12,885	10,395	80.68	2,490	19.32
74	10,353	8,295	80.12	2,058	19.88	118	13,359	10,628	79.56	2,731	20.44
75	10,360	8,402	81.10	1,958	18.90	119	13,498	11,002	81.51	2,496	18.49
76	10,534	8,442	80.14	2,092	19.86	120	14,134	11,200	79.24	2,934	20.76
77	10,465	8,289	79.21	2,176	20.79	121	14,672	11,765	80.19	2,907	19.81
78	10,705	8,498	79.38	2,207	20.62	122	14,688	11,719	79.79	2,969	20.21
79	10,679	8,401	78.67	2,278	21.33	123	14,420	11,717	81.26	2,703	18.74
80	10,522	8,170	77.65	2,352	22.35	124	14,519	11,706	80.63	2,813	19.37
81	10,653	8,460	79.41	2,193	20.59	125	14,657	11,719	79.95	2,938	20.05
82	10,653	8,535	80.12	2,118	19.88	126	14,905	12,064	80.94	2,841	19.06
83	10,648	8,436	79.23	2,212	20.77	127	15,040	12,376	82.29	2,664	17.71
84	10,821	8,546	78.98	2,275	21.02	128	15,201	12,155	79.96	3,046	20.04
85	10,748	8,491	79.00	2,257	21.00	129	15,045	11,951	79.44	3,094	20.56
86	10,745	8,387	78.05	2,358	21.95	130	15,533	12,668	81.56	2,865	18.44
87	11,375	8,825	77.58	2,550	22.42	131	15,711	12,936	82.34	2,775	17.66
88	11,462	8,961	78.18	2,501	21.82	132	15,336	12,513	81.59	2,823	18.41
89	11,633	8,902	76.52	2,731	23.48	133	15,249	12,215	80.10	3,034	19.90
90	11,842	9,280	78.36	2,562	21.64	134	15,326	12,416	81.01	2,910	18.99
91	11,856	9,409	79.36	2,447	20.64	135	15,606	12,895	82.63	2,711	17.37
92	11,869	9,384	79.06	2,485	20.94	136	15,247	12,312	80.75	2,935	19.25
93	12,203	9,794	80.26	2,409	19.74	137	14,695	12,042	81.95	2,653	18.05
94	12,638	10,117	80.05	2,521	19.95	138	15,063	11,920	79.13	3,143	20.87
95	12,846	10,338	80.48	2,508	19.52	139	15,481	12,666	81.82	2,815	18.18
96	13,019	10,611	81.50	2,408	18.50	140	15,628	12,842	82.17	2,786	17.83
97	12,889	10,380	80.53	2,509	19.47	141	15,554	12,768	82.09	2,786	17.91
98	13,305	10,903	81.95	2,402	18.05	142	15,181	12,194	80.32	2,987	19.68
99	13,778	11,157	80.98	2,621	19.02	143	14,494	11,652	80.39	2,842	19.61
100	13,726	11,118	81.00	2,608	19.00	144	14,598	11,601	79.47	2,997	20.53
101	14,064	11,129	79.13	2,935	20.87	145	15,530	12,352	79.54	3,178	20.46
102	13,259	10,185	76.82	3,074	23.18	146	15,940	12,765	80.08	3,175	19.92
103	13,654	10,787	79.00	2,867	21.00	147	16,346	13,145	80.42	3,201	19.58
104	14,018	11,043	78.78	2,975	21.22	148	16,730	13,568	81.10	3,162	18.90
105	13,492	10,748	79.66	2,744	20.34	149	16,989	13,779	81.11	3,210	18.89
106	13,878	10,809	77.89	3,069	22.11	150	17,148	13,740	80.13	3,408	19.87
107	13,665	10,681	78.16	2,984	21.84	151	17,222	13,851	80.45	3,371	19.55
108	13,624	10,700	78.54	2,924	21.46	152	17,434	13,813	79.23	3,621	20.77
109	13,858	11,109	80.16	2,749	19.84	153	15,297	12,386	80.97	2,911	19.03
110	13,958	11,367	81.44	2,591	18.56	154	15,353	12,325	80.28	3,028	19.72
111	13,865	10,525	75.91	3,340	24.09	155	15,168	11,883	78.34	3,285	21.66
112	14,086	11,499	81.63	2,587	18.37	156	15,145	11,747	77.56	3,398	22.44
113	14,054	11,026	78.45	3,028	21.55	157	15,155	11,851	78.20	3,304	21.80
114	13,758	10,924	79.40	2,834	20.60	158	14,565	11,506	79.00	3,059	21.00
115	12,916	10,351	80.14	2,565	19.86	159	13,928	11,123	79.86	2,805	20.14
116	13,397	10,875	81.17	2,522	18.83						

The accompanying diagrams show, graphically, the percentage of distribution by color of the total number of employees of this company by weeks, from January, 1916, to January, 1919, and the percentage of white and colored employees by weeks during this same period.

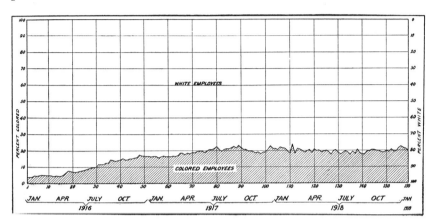

COMPARATIVE INCREASE IN PERCENTAGE AMONG WHITE AND COLORED EMPLOYEES IN ONE MEAT-PACKING PLANT DURING A PERIOD OF 159 WEEKS.

The third piece of evidence came from a steel company at Indiana Harbor, Ind., and shows the total number and per cent of white and colored employees from January, 1918, through December of the same year. This shows a total, at the beginning of the period, of 2,020 employees, of which 1,736, or 85.94 per cent, were white, and 284, or 14.06 per cent, were colored. At the close of the period the firm was employing a total of 2,171 employees, of which 1,681, or 77.43 per cent, were white, and 490, or 22.57 per cent, were colored. The number of colored employees showed a steady increase over the original number, running as high as 538 in October, 1918, to the closing number at the end of December, which number showed a considerable increase in total colored employees and a corresponding increased percentage of the total number of employees. Other discussions of workers in iron and steel have been given in Chapter VI.

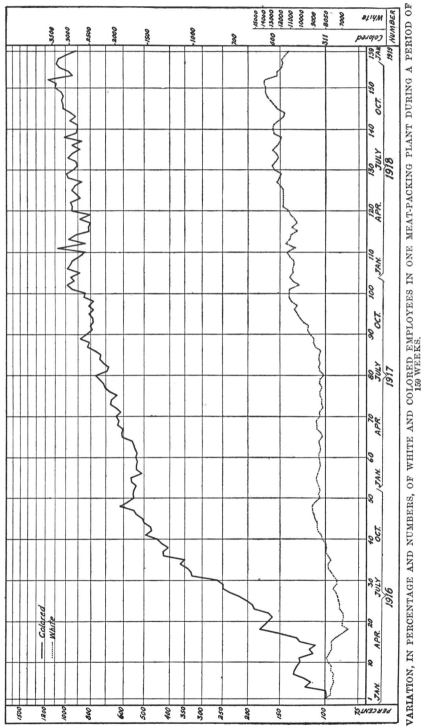

VARIATION, IN PERCENTAGE AND NUMBERS, OF WHITE AND COLORED EMPLOYEES IN ONE MEAT-PACKING PLANT DURING A PERIOD OF 159 WEEKS.

CHAPTER VIII.

NEGRO LABOR IN THE UNITED STATES SHIPYARDS.

The widespread demand for ships to "beat" the unlawful submarine warfare of the Germans led the Nation to see that ships were needed to win the war. The building of ships called for labor of all kinds, skilled, semiskilled, and unskilled, and those who responded to build ships were serving the cause no less than those who responded for service in the Army. During the war the Negroes showed their patriotism in this particular fully as they did in others. In the shipyards under the jurisdiction of the United States Shipping Board— Emergency Fleet Corporation—covering four shipbuilding districts on the Atlantic coast, one on the Gulf coast, two on the Pacific coast, and one in the Great Lakes district, there were 24,648 Negroes employed during the war and 14,075 employed up to September, 1919, following the signing of the armistice. In the southern district during the war there were 11,991 and for the period after the war 5,504; in the middle Atlantic district there were 4,506 and 5,223, respectively; in the Delaware River district, 5,165 and 2,230, respectively; in the northern Atlantic district, 371 and 297, respectively; in the Gulf district, 1,830 and 309, respectively; in the southern Pacific district, 582 and 399, respectively; in the northern Pacific district, 176 and 96, respectively; and in the Great Lakes district, 27 and 17, respectively. Both the numbers involved and the distribution of the numbers, both during the war and the months following the signing of the armistice, give ample evidence that Negroes played a large part in the building of the ships. Unfortunately, it has not been feasible to secure the figures of the white workmen under the United States Shipping Board for these districts.

We do have, however, a full record of the occupations in which Negro workmen were engaged. During the war 4,963, or about 20.7 per cent, were engaged in occupations which may be classed as skilled occupations, leaving 19,685, or about 80 per cent, in unskilled occupations, some of which could probably be classed as semiskilled occupations. After the war 3,872, or 27.47 per cent, were in skilled occupations and 10,203, or 72.53 per cent, in unskilled occupations, some of which may be classed as semiskilled. It is significant that the largest number of Negroes in skilled occupations both in steel and wooden ship construction was in the southern district, both during and after the war. The second largest during the war was in the Delaware River district and after the war in the middle Atlantic district.

Negroes participated in 46 of the 55 separate shipbuilding occupations listed during the war period, and in 49 such occupations after the war. In addition, during the war 21 occupations had less than 10 Negroes employed and after the war 17 occupations had less than 10 Negroes employed in them. This leaves 25 occupations with 10 or more Negroes during the war and 22 occupations with 10 or more Negroes employed after the war.

The details are given in full in the accompanying table, but some illuminating comparisons may be made here. During the war there were 1,464 Negro carpenters, 225 calkers, 21 chippers and calkers, 631 fasteners, 11 blacksmiths, 102 blacksmiths' helpers, 36 riggers, 38 riveters, 22 foremen, 240 drillers and reamers, 399 bolters. These all are important skilled or semiskilled occupations in the building of ships. After the war there were only 74 carpenters, 59 calkers, 36 chippers and calkers, 143 fasteners, 7 blacksmiths, 45 blacksmiths' helpers, and 191 reamers and drillers. There were, however, 49 riveters and 1,116 bolters, these occupations showing increases.

The analysis of these figures indicates that in the more highly skilled and therefore the more highly paid occupations there has been a greater decrease in the number of Negroes in the shipyards than in the less skilled or semiskilled occupations, but taking the skilled and semiskilled occupations together, Negro workers held their numbers and showed less decrease after the war than they did in the unskilled occupations, altogether, after the war. The total decrease after the war of Negroes in all skilled or semiskilled occupations was only 20.7 per cent, while the total decrease after the war of Negro workers in the unskilled occupations was about 48 per cent, or nearly one-half. While these figures show a very decided decrease in the more highly skilled occupations, on the whole they make a favorable showing for Negro workmen in the shipbuilding industry, both during and after the war.

Not only did Negroes enter the skilled and semiskilled occupations during the war in large numbers but they remained in these occupations in larger proportions than in the unskilled occupations.

The following table shows in detail the number of Negro employees working in skilled and unskilled occupations at shipbuilding plants under the jurisdiction of the United States Shipping Board—Emergency Fleet Corporation—during and after the war in the eight principal shipyard districts, during 1918 and 1919. The skilled and semiskilled workers were not classified separately in the available record. The full details showing number of Negroes employed in the eight principal shipyard districts in specified occupations during and after the war are given in the following table:

TABLE VI.—*Negro employees working at plants under the jurisdiction of the United States Shipping Board—Emergency Fleet Corporation—during and after the war, in the eight principal shipyard districts, 1918-19.*[1]

[Columns 1, during the war; columns 2, after the war.]

Kind of Occupation.[2]	Southern district.		Middle Atlantic district.		Delaware River district.[3]		Northern Atlantic district.		Gulf district.		Southern Pacific district.		Northern Pacific district.		Great Lakes district.		Total.[6]		Grand total.
	1	2	1	2	1	2	1	2	1	2	1	2	1	2	1	2	1	2	
Total number employed[4]	11,991	5,504	4,506	5,223	[5]5,165	[5]2,230	371	297	1,830	309	582	399	176	96	27	17	24,648	14,075	38,723
Skilled	3,578	3,078	117	114	5,165	99	258	218	541	109	309	171	140	72	20	11	4,963	3,872	8,835
Unskilled	8,413	2,426	4,389	5,109	5,165	2,131	113	79	1,289	200	273	227	36	25	7	6	19,685	10,203	29,888
Back-handlers	8	21															8	21	29
Blacksmiths	11	5															11	7	18
Blacksmiths' helpers	99	44							2								102	45	147
Bolters	130	955				3	98	85			166	69			5	4	399	1,116	1,515
Bolters' learners		138																138	138
Carpenters	1,367	64	35	1			13	7	46				3	2			1,464	74	1,538
Calkers	182	21	17	28			26	10								1	225	60	285
Calkers and chippers	17	35					3				1						21	36	57
Cementers	2	29									1						3	29	32
Cleaners		31					3	5			72	21					75	57	132
Cranemen	48	7				3											48	10	58
Dockmen	37	36															37	36	73
Drillers and reamers	50	125	4	23			43	41	140						3	2	240	191	431
Engineers	10	1	1				1										12	1	13
Erectors	13	12										3					13	15	28
Fasteners	303	60	5	3		10	6	1	316	69							631	143	774
Firemen	87	37	2	2		13			27	8							116	60	176
Foremen	22	10				1											22	11	33
Furnacemen	9	22				1											9	23	32
General helpers	556	328	53	56		49	1	8	8	21	8	13	126	63	1	1	744	538	1,282
Handymen	200	297	53	1			7	7	2	2		3	1	2	2	1	204	303	507
Heaters	52	238															69	249	318
Hewsers	5	11															5	11	16
Holders-on	88	220					15	22					2	3	2	1	115	247	362
Hookers-on																		13	13
Oilmen		4				2			10	9		4					33	21	54
Passers	54	134					6	8			33	19					66	147	213
Punchers	11	22									6	2					11	22	33
Riggers	23	15					9	1			3	4	1				36	20	56

Riveters	25	69	.....	.....	10	7	.....	23	.....	3	.....	38	99	137
Stage builders	.....	.....	.....	.....	.....	.....	.....	9	.....	.....	.....	13	.....	13
Steel construction	150	70	.....	.....	4	.....	.....	.....	1	.....	.....	150	70	220
All other occupations	19	17	17	13	14	9	9	1	2	1	43	59	102	

1 This table has been reconstructed from a previous table prepared by the U. S. Shipping Board.

2 Includes both wood and steel ship occupations.

3 Includes agencies not directly in the Delaware River district, but under its jurisdiction.

4 The figures against this item include every kind of occupation in which Negroes were employed, as reported by the United States Shipping Board, and should not be presumed to be the totals for the kinds of occupations listed in the first column, which include only such representative occupations as are deemed of particular significance, and, therefore, of practicable value for tabulation.

5 During the war Delaware River district workers were not classified by occupations, but after the war agency workers of this district were classified.

6 Itemized totals are for skilled workers only.

RECORD-BREAKING NEGRO WORKERS.

How a Negro pile-driver gained the world's pile-driving record is told, partially in his own language, as follows:

WORLD'S PILE-DRIVING RECORD SMASHED.

Edward Burwell, the Negro pile-driving captain whose Negro crew of 11 men broke the world's record in driving piles on shipway No. 46 (Philadelphia, Pa.), was asked how he came to break the standing record. Burwell smiled and pointed to a placard nailed on the pile-driving machine. The placard read: "If at first you don't succeed, try, try, again."

The record prior to Burwell's wonderful drive was 165 piles in 9 hours. Burwell and his crew drove 220 65-foot piles in 9 hours and 5 minutes, and a good part of the time the crew worked in a terrific downpour of rain. Since coming on the job in January, 1918, Burwell's crew has driven 4,141 piles with a total of 241,573 linear feet. The crew under Burwell is employed by the Arthur McMullen Co. This company had the contract to drive 21,434 piles. Burwell and his crew drove about 20 per cent of this number.

"I went into the pile-driving business 15 years ago," Burwell said in speaking of his new record. "I was never on a job as large as this one before. It was due to rivalry between another Negro foreman and myself that I made up my mind to go after the record of 165 piles held by another company.

"The sign filled our crew with enthusiasm. We decided, one night, that a new world's record would be made on the morrow, and it was. Of course, we had our little mechanical troubles, and instead of fretting and fuming, the men just glanced at the sign and started in with renewed vigor and the record was smashed."

Capt. Burwell then produced the log of the crew on the day the world's record was made. It is rather interesting reading and is printed below:

Piles driven.

7 a. m. to 8 a. m. 27
8 a. m. to 9 a. m. 23
    (Delay 4½ minutes due to broken steam line; raining very hard
      from 8.15 to 10 a. m.)
9 a. m. to 10 a. m. 28
10 a. m. to 11 a. m. 22
    (Delay 8 minutes due to pile fall breaking.)
11 a. m. to 12 a. m. 27
12 noon to 12.30 p. m. (lunch).
12.30 p. m. to 1.30 p. m. 25
    (Heavy rain with electric showers from 1.25 to 2.50 p. m., and from
      1.25 to 1.40 p. m. air pressure dropped considerably, which held
      up hammer.)
1.30 p. m. to 2.30 p. m. 23
2.30 p. m. to 3.30 p. m. 23
3.30 p. m. to 4.35 p. m. 22

Total, 9 hours and 5 minutes. 220

Note.—Total linear feet of piles, 14,260. Previous world's record, 165 piles in 9 hours and 15 minutes.

Of no less interest is the performance of a gang of Negro riveters working at Sparrows Point, Md., in the plant of the Bethlehem Steel Corporation, in breaking the world's record for driving rivets. One of the gang, Charles Knight, drove 4,875 three-quarter-inch rivets in a 9-hour day. The previous highest record was 4,442, made by a workman in a Scottish shipyard. Mr. Knight is a highly respectable and industrious citizen of Baltimore, Md., and a native of Virginia.

CHAPTER IX.

REPORT OF WORK IN FLORIDA AND GEORGIA.

FLORIDA.

On July 16, 1918, Hon. Sidney J. Catts, governor of Florida, called together representatives of Negro citizens from all parts of the State at Jacksonville, who, with about 15 of Florida's most representative white employers, met for a day's conference on the labor situation in the State. After a thorough discussion the governor authorized the conference to work out plans with the representatives of the Department of Labor for the organization of the State, county, and city Negro workers' advisory committees. The governor, as chairman of the State council of defense, accepted the honorary chairmanship of the committee, and with the executive secretary of the council a plan was worked out so that the colored members appointed on the Negro workers' advisory committees had white members from the county councils of defense to act on these committees as cooperating members. In this way, in a short time there were developed these cooperative relationships between white and colored representatives through the Negro workers' advisory committees in 26 counties in the State, including the important city centers such as Jacksonville, Tampa, Miami, and Pensacola.

The following letters show the spirit and action of the council of defense, the governor, and other interested parties:

STATE OF FLORIDA,
EXECUTIVE CHAMBER,
Tallahassee, July 31, 1918.

Dr. GEO. E. HAYNES,
Department of Labor, Washington, D. C.

DEAR SIR: I have your letter inclosing list of colored citizens nominated at a conference held in Jacksonville, and also copy of their constitution.

I thank you for the same and will give it my attention. I am willing to cooperate with your race in every way possible.

With best wishes, I am
Yours, very truly,

(Signed)   SIDNEY J. CATTS, *Governor.*

STATE COUNCIL OF DEFENSE,
Tallahassee, Fla., October 29, 1918.

Dr. GEO. E. HAYNES,
Director of Negro Economics, Washington, D. C.

DEAR SIR: Yours of the 21st instant, addressed to his excellency Gov. Sidney J. Catts, relative to the work of your advisory committee, together with your request for the cooperation of county councils of defense has been referred to me for reply.

Replying, beg to advise that at the meeting of our advisory committee October 25, inst., this matter was brought before the committee, and it was agreed to give your committee the assistance in the capacity requested.

Yours, very truly,

(Signed)   H. S. HOWARD,
Executive Secretary.

Following the State conference and the appointment of the State Negro workers' advisory committee, upon the recommendation of a number of white and colored citizens, W. A. Armwood, of Tampa, Fla., a graduate of the State college, who had been a successful carpenter and contractor and at that time was principal of the colored public school at Tampa and successfully conducting a drug business of his own, was chosen as supervisor of Negro economics for Florida. He had known many workmen in all parts of the State and very soon was in touch with them in various districts. It was due to his untiring effort that many of the activities of the State were developed.

One of the first steps taken following the organization of committees was to give Negro workers wholesome advice about the necessity of continued and systematic work during the period of the war for the production of such commodities as were necessary to win it. Two methods were used for such advice: First, circular letters and bulletins were sent out to the members of the county and city committees touching upon various points for stimulating the morale and efficiency of workers in the different localities of the State. Second, a series of mass meetings of white and colored citizens was planned and carried out in the early fall, following the conference. The Director of Negro Economics was present at a number of these meetings and both white and colored citizens attended in large numbers. There were usually white and colored speakers before the audience on the same platform.

One significant service rendered by the State Negro workers' advisory committee was to correct a misapprehension and feeling that was growing due to the spread of rumor among employers that Negro women workers in large numbers were receiving governmental allotments from male relatives in the Army and were taking advantage of this money to refuse to engage in any useful occupation. The committee made a careful State-wide investigation of the facts and found that the rumor was groundless. Wide publicity was given to the actual facts of the patriotic work being done by colored women throughout the State, and this served to allay feeling and friction.

Following is a summary of the other work carried out by the committee:

1. Educational campaigns were carried out in the 26 counties, in various cities of the State, at mass meetings and at the regular gatherings of Negro churches, lodges, and other organizations to inform Negro workers of the necessity of steady and reliable service to keep up production for winning the war, to promote prosperity, and to improve the relations between the races.

2. Cooperation was given to the United States Employment Service in the securing and placement of thousands of Negro workers and in the placement of returning soldiers.

3. Misunderstandings were adjusted through advisory conferences of employers and employees and county officials. This work was carried on in the case of both individual workers and employers as well as organizations, and in this way the stoppage of work was prevented.

4. By conferences with State and county officials and cooperation with the State council of defense, local officials were induced to use the good offices of the Negro workers' advisory committees in persuading Negro workers to work steadily and with enthusiasm. This method was found more effective than the application of compulsory labor regulations advocated by many.

5. Working conditions were improved in many plants voluntarily by employers after conferences and suggestions either from the Supervisor of Negro Economics or from members of the advisory committees. In most cases these conferences were sought in the first instance by the employers.

6. The health conditions of Negro workers were improved through the advice to both employers and workers on methods of protecting their health. Advertising material and literature along these lines were given out.

7. Besides the cooperation of the State council of defense and the governor of the State, as shown by the preceding correspondence, the following organizations and agencies gave full support to the work in the State: State Agricultural and Mechanical College for Negroes; State Federation of Colored Women's Clubs; local organizations of the Negro National Business League; local lodges; and churches of the several denominations.

GEORGIA.

On August 9, 1918, a conference of about 75 representative colored men met in Atlanta, Ga., in response to an official invitation issued by Hon. Hugh M. Dorsey, governor of the State, that they assemble to confer with representatives of the Department of Labor and of the State commission of labor on matters relating to Negro labor. After an all-day session, Judge Price Gilbert, of the Supreme Court and of the State council of defense, met the conference representing the governor and the council of defense. In the course of an interesting all-day session going over the situation of the State and the plans of the Department of Labor, the conference recommended and adopted an outline of an organization of the State, county, and city Negro workers' advisory committees along lines of those set up in other States. The report adopted by the special committee contained the following recommendations:

We, your committee on plans and work, beg leave to render the following report:

First, we recommend that a chairman be designated for each county by this body and that said chairman appoint a committee of nine from different sections of said county to work with him in coordinating the work of his county.

Second, that a series of public meetings be held in prominent places, such as churches, lodge rooms, etc., in said counties, under the supervision of said committees and that said committees be requested to invite some of the leading white citizens of their respective communities to participate in said meetings.

Third, we recommend plans for labor demonstrations and parades to be made for January 1, 1919.

Fourth, that said county committee get in touch with a number of open minded, patriotic white citizens in their respective communities to the end that through them the general public may be informed about the doings of the State Negro workers' advisory committee.

Fifth, as a means of recruiting labor in the various communities in our State, we recommend (1) that laborers be guaranteed protection as citizens; (2) that better housing and sanitation conditions be provided; (3) ample school facilities with competent and well-paid teachers; (4) pay commensurate with services rendered for laborers; (5) better transportation and equal accommodations on the railroads; in short, make labor satisfied and labor will remain.

Respectfully,

E. P. Johnson,	G. B. Burney
H. A. Rucker,	H. R. Butler,
J. P. Davis,	J. Q. Gasset,
E. J. Turner,	Mrs. Londie Andrews.
C. E. Williams.	

After the meeting of the State Conference of Georgia, Prof. H. A. Hunt, principal of the Fort Valley High and Industrial School, was appointed as supervisor of Negro economics of the State. Associated with him as examiner in the United States Employment Service for activity over the State was Mr. Rufus P. Bennett, who assisted the Federal Director of the United States Employment Service and Prof. Hunt in many of the difficult problems relating mainly to agricultural labor in this large State.

CHAPTER X.

REPORT OF WORK IN ILLINOIS.

In the early development of the plans of the department for the Division of Negro Economics it seemed feasible that one man should advise on policies and plans for one district comprising Michigan and Illinois. As the work developed this district was divided into the two States, Michigan and Illinois.

At the beginning in June, 1918, Mr. Forrester B. Washington, of Detroit, Mich., was appointed as supervisor of Negro economics in the district comprising Michigan and Illinois. It had been estimated by the department that about 30,000 Negro migrants had moved into Detroit and that probably 50,000 had come into the Chicago district within the period during 1917 and 1918. Mr. Washington, trained at Tufts College and the New York School of Philanthropy, had had three years' experience and unusual success as executive secretary of the Detroit Urban League in cooperation with the Employers' Association of Detroit in handling the industrial problems growing out of the influx of the thousands of Negro newcomers.

During July and August, he very successfully dealt with these problems of his district, which centered mainly at Detroit and Chicago. About September 1, Michigan and Illinois were made separate districts and Mr. Washington was transferred to Chicago and began the intensive development of the work in Illinois. He began with a study of the communities of the State where large numbers of Negroes resided and arranged for a State conference, which was held Monday, September 30, 1918, at Springfield, in the old historic Sangamon County courthouse, so well known in relation to the revered memory of Abraham Lincoln. Delegates representing Negro workers, white employers, and white workers were present from 14 points in the State. They spent a day in discussing general conditions and adopted the form of organization of a State advisory committee with local committees. In the weeks that followed the conference, Negro workers' advisory committees were formed in 17 counties and 9 cities throughout the State to deal with the many delicate and difficult labor problems. Some of the results of the activity under the supervision of Mr. Washington are outlined in the following pages.

During sessions of the conference several committees were appointed and made reports, among them the committee on general conditions, which gave such a concrete review of the relationships between Negro workers and white workers and white employers that a greater part of the report is included as follows:

We, your committee on general conditions as to labor and general war work relating to Negroes in the State of Illinois, beg leave to submit the following report:

First. We find that the city of Chicago is the greatest center of Negro influx on account of the conditions produced by the war of any community in the State of Illinois; and that the cities of East St. Louis, Cairo, Springfield, and Peoria follow in their order. The city of Decatur does not have the same condition as does the cities above named, neither does the city of Danville, nor Quincy, as they are governed in some degree by local conditions which have to do with only their own particular vicinities.

We find that in the mining districts in southern Illinois, composing the counties of St. Clair, Perry, Jackson, Franklin, and Williamson and adjacent counties, the conditions of the colored miners as to housing and economic conditions are on par with those of the white miners. In fact, all mining districts of the State are guided by the miners' union, and the purpose of the leaders of the miners, and of the mine owners as well in those districts, seems to have been directed to the task of winning the war by doing and giving effective service and every effort has been lent to neutralizing the opposing forces that both white and colored workers may understand and help each other and in this way work for a common purpose.

OTHER LABOR.

In Chicago, at the stockyards, we find that conditions are much improved and better relations created by organization. The colored men and workers and the white brother in toil have been brought together.

In the other parts of Illinois we find that the Negro as a laborer is not understood. The white men have been led to believe that the Negro was his common industrial enemy and as a result some very grave disturbances have taken place, such as the recent one at East St. Louis.

In many instances ill feelings have resulted in the employers suffering from shortages of effective workers and the propagandists of German connection have, no doubt, seized upon this spirit of unrest to further their wicked ends and many instances of this spirit have fallen within the knowledge of some of the members of your committee. Some employers have misunderstood, in that they had been led to believe that Negroes were not faithful nor yet effective workers, but that notion has been pushed into the discard and now, thanks to the work of the Department of Labor and the leaders of the various organizations having these matters at heart, Negroes are entering all the avenues of endeavor.

Some of the cities above mentioned are not cursed with the bad conditions above complained of. We are pleased to refer to the city of Decatur as a city where the best of relations exist between white and colored people and in the large factories of that city. They work side by side in harmony, and general helpfulness results from that condition.

In the capital city of Illinois (Springfield) for many years colored workers have not been given employment in many of the factories; but, owing to conditions brought about by the war, a sign of betterment is seen. Now some of the steam laundries are finding colored workers a decided success. A watch factory has increased its quota of colored workers, but we find that in many of the factories the closed door stands between the colored worker and employment. Your committee is driven to the conclusion that in many instances the lack of efficiency on the part of the workers who apply, the lack of attention to duty, the lack of thrift and energetic effort is proving the undoing of the colored workers.

RÉSUMÉ.

We recommend that steps be taken to educate both the colored and white toiler to the fact that the interest of both the white and colored toiler and of their employers as well is finally centralized only in the finished products of their toil when it is ready for the markets of the world. We further recommend that an effort be made to bring the Negro workers of the country into a closer relationship with the employers of labor of the State of Illinois and at the same time with the various labor organizations of this State in order that the interests of all parties, namely, white workers, colored workers, and employers of labor, and the trade-union as a medium of conciliation and arbitration, may all be conserved, remembering at all times that the supreme and centralizing efforts of every American citizen should be, and is, winning the war.

Respectfully submitted by your committee.

GEO. W. FORD, *Chairman.*
HUGH SINGLETON.
J. B. OSBY.
GEO. W. BUCKNER.
A. K. FOOTE.
CHAS. S. GIBBS.

The situation in southwestern Illinois, particularly the East St. Louis situation, was so vital with the whole question of Negro labor and war production in this territory that the department soon found it necessary to have the supervisor of Negro economics give attention to St. Louis and to territory in the State of Missouri in further work to adjust relations of Negro workers and white workers. Accordingly, at the request of the Federal director for Missouri of the United States Employment Service, the department called a conference of Negro workers, white employers, and white workers, which was held at St. Louis, Mo., December 18, 1918. An interesting incident in connection with this conference was that it was held in the Poro Building, a new structure just completed by a Negro corporation of unusual success. The conference was attended by select delegates from about 12 centers throughout the State and its significance is shown by the program of work attached.

PROGRAM OF WORK ADOPTED BY THE MISSOURI CONFERENCE ON PROBLEMS OF NEGRO LABOR, DECEMBER 18, 1918.

1. Race relations.
    a. This committee should take steps to get white and colored labor together in order to better understand the ideals and ambitions of each.
        1. Negro labor leaders shall be urged to teach their people that their interests are common with those of white labor.
        2. White labor leaders shall be urged to teach their people that their interests are common with those of colored labor and also instruct them regarding the high standard of living of Negroes.
2. Release of Negro labor.
    a. Steps should be taken to prevent wholesale discharge of Negroes in order not to cause race friction.
        1. Visits should be made by representatives of the local committee to factories where they seem to be discharging Negroes wholesale.
        2. Visits should be made by representatives of the committee to factories where large numbers of Negroes are employed, urging that the latter be discharged only in the same proportion and for the same reason that employees of other races are discharged.
3. Housing.
    a. This committee should make plans to house returning colored soldiers.
        1. By establishing a room registry for colored soldiers in the various communities.
        2. The Government shall be urged to grant land to those returning colored soldiers who desire to settle in the agricultural districts.
    b. The local committee will urge employers that they provide their colored employees with housing that is sanitary.
4. Make plans to create openings for Negroes.
    a. By investigating every public construction program and ascertaining whether or not Negroes are to be used.
    b. By encouraging Negroes to go into business for themselves.
5. Distribution of labor.
    a. Prevent unequal distribution of Negroes through exchange of information re shortage or surplus of colored labor by committeemen from various localities.
    b. Cooperate with the nearest United States Employment Service office.
6. Act as agency representing the Negro in soldiers' bureaus—about to be established by the United States Government.
7. Cooperation of agencies.
    This committee shall seek to develop cooperation in the carrying out of its program from—
        a. Labor union.
        b. Philanthropic agencies.
        c. Churches.
        d. Lodges.
        e. Employers' organizations.

8. Education.
    a. Negro.
        1. Shop talks on efficiency.
        2. Lectures in colored churches and fraternal organizations on efficiency.
        3. Neighborhood visits on better living.
        4. Special attention shall be paid to the encouragement of thrift.
    b. White employer.
        1. Employers should be furnished with information re Negro's efficiency.

It may be added that local committees were set up in this State in only four places, as the restriction of activities developed in this direction commenced a few weeks after this conference. It should be added, however, that Missouri offers in many places one of the most important fields where Negro labor may be more efficient and where there is a necessity for developing better understanding between white workers, white employers, and Negro workers. A large part of the unskilled labor in the industrial districts in St. Louis and some mining and coal districts make this matter of interest to all, both employees and employers in this city.

The supervisor of Negro ecomomics for Illinois, following the State conference at Springfield, quickly lined up his work with the private agencies and organizations in various parts of the State. Consequently each city and county Negro workers' advisory committee was able to bring to its assistance the cooperation of many white and colored citizens; so that despite subsequent racial disturbances in Chicago it may justly be said that much friction, both in Chicago and elsewhere, was removed by this cordial effort of advisory committees and local organizations. In fact, in three places—one of them East St. Louis—acute racial situations were met and adjusted through this means. One of the first pieces of work was to ascertain the firms employing colored workers, so as to give some substantial idea of the extent to which they were employed. The list included some of the largest firms in Illinois, the number of firms in each locality being as follows:

Abingdon	1	Hoopston	1
Alton	2	Indiana Harbor	1
Aurora	2	Madison	1
Batavia	1	Moline	4
Bloomington	1	Morris	1
Cairo	6	Murphysboro	1
Canton	1	Onarga	1
Herrin	1	Paris	1
Chicago	89	Peoria	6
Chicago Heights	5	Quincy	4
Danville	2	Rochelle	1
Decatur	1	Rock Island	3
Dixon	1	Rockford	8
East Moline	2	Rockdale	1
East St. Louis	12	Granite City	1
Freeport	4	East St. Louis	1
Granite City	3	Springfield	1
St. Louis	2	Sycamore	1
Hammond	1	Waukegan	2
Harvey	6	North Chicago	1
West Harvey	1		

The tables and discussion found elsewhere—giving experience of Negro workers in industrial plants, showing wages, conditions, and other pertinent facts—include some of these firms in Illinois.

Of particular significance was the work in Illinois of assisting in the placement in civilian occupations the returning Negro soldiers and sailors. General cooperation in Illinois in the matter of caring for these returning men was well organized. Such organizations as the Red Cross, the Y. M. C. A., the Knights of Columbus, the Jewish Welfare Board, the Chicago Urban League, and many other agencies cooperated effectively and closely with the United States Employment Service, the supervisor of Negro economics, and the State employment office. The State employment service and the United States Employment Service, immediately following the signing of the armistice, adopted the plans of the Federal service for meeting needs of the returning soldiers by the establishment of placement bureaus with the cooperation of private organizations, some of which are named above. In addition to the returning soldiers, many workers had been released from war industries. This complicated the labor situation in Chicago and other points in Illinois in the months following the signing of the armistice, and required the most delicate handling in the most sympathetic manner. With the hearty cooperation of the Washington office the plans went forward rapidly, and the work was undertaken in the placement of the 10,000 Negro soldiers who returned to Chicago. In addition to the central office, a special bureau was opened on the South Side of Chicago, in the main district containing large numbers of Negro residents in professions and profitable enterprises.

In conducting this special office, however, no restriction was made limiting it to the use of colored soldiers. Its sole purpose was to put the placement facilities within the easiest reach of those whom it was designed to serve. An appeal letter signed by a central committee representing a number of welfare agencies and the Federal Government was sent to over 5,000 employers in Chicago urging especially that they give attention to employment of members of the Eighth Illinois Regiment just returned from service overseas. This letter was approved by the State Advisory Board of the Employment Service, the executive committee of the Soldiers' and Sailors' Bureau, and the Federal director, United States Employment Service. In addition, a sort of flying squadron of returning soldiers in uniform was sent throughout the city to solicit opportunities for these men. The success of this effort as a part of the general response may be judged from the fact that, although there was rather an acute unemployment situation in Chicago at the time, it was not many weeks before the situation had been cleared up and the supervisor reported that it was possible to say that a job could be found for every man that really wanted work. As an example of the activities in the placement of returning Negro soldiers, the following figures for one week are given: Attendance, 468; registrations, 198; help wanted, 152; referred, 156; reported placed, 114; transferred, 26.

Although the following figures were included in the report of the United States Employment Service the following report of the South Side office during the month of May, 1918, is given, as it had more placements than any other office in Chicago for that month:

Men.—Attendance, 1,430; registration, 795; help wanted, 824; referred, 637; reported placed, 570; transferred, 3.

In all this work special mention should be made of the assistance given by private organizations, especially the Chicago Urban League, which maintained an employment office in cooperation with the United States Employment Service and the State employment service throughout the period of the United States Employment Service work in the city of Chicago.

One of the special forms of the work in Illinois was to assist in the improvement of depressing housing conditions in the State. When the plans of the United States Homes Registration Service had developed to the point that a field worker was needed in this territory, the supervisor of Negro economics canvassed urban localities in Illinois. Chicago, East St. Louis, Springfield, Quincy, Alton, Cairo, Peoria, Bloomington, Centralia, Decatur, Danville, Jacksonville, and Monmouth were covered by the Negro workers' advisory committees at each point. Through the assistance of these committees, the field agent of the Homes Registration Service and the Illinois supervisor of Negro economics formulated plans for a campaign on housing. These plans suffered curtailment due to a change in plans of the housing bureau.

As a means of developing stability of labor and thrift among Negro workers, a study was made of cooperative store enterprises, and the laws governing same. Thereafter plans of organization were outlined giving details as to incorporation, stock values, share and loan of capital, stock holders' meetings, duties of boards of directors, management, buying of goods, bookkeeping auditing of accounts, dividends and surplus earnings, and similar details. The results of this study were issued in mimeographed form and put into the hands of Negro workers' advisory committeemen for State-wide distribution. So valuable does this outline seem that it is given in full as follows:

116 NORTH DEARBORN STREET,
Chicago, Ill., June 17, 1919.

[From the supervisor of Negro economics in Illinois to the Negro Workers Advisory Committee on the subject of cooperative stores.]

One of the lines along which the Director of Negro Economics is laying great emphasis is that of the development of business enterprises among our people. Because of the small number of Negroes who handle any large amount of capital the most successful business enterprises among colored people must necessarily be cooperative.

I am sending you to-day a brief outline of the method of starting and carrying on a cooperative store.

Cooperative stores have been very successful in a great many places in this country and enormously successful in Europe.

Already a cooperative store conducted by Negroes is on foot in Illinois. It is being promoted by the members of Butcher Workmen's Local 651 of Chicago.

It seems to me that there are enough colored people in your community to support such a store.

Too much of the money that is being earned by the colored group at present remains in their hands only for a short time; then goes to the hands of others, usually foreign born of short residence in this country.

A cooperative store planned and carried on by Negroes will mean that a large portion of the money earned by Negroes will be kept within the group.

Further information can be obtained by writing to the Supervisor of Negro Economics in Illinois or to the Department of Agriculture, Washington, D. C., for Bulletin 394 on cooperative stores, price 10 cents, or to Mr. Duncan McDonald, secretary-treasurer, Central States Cooperative Society, Springfield, Ill., who has issued some very interesting pamphlets on this subject at a small cost of not over 5 cents.

Very truly, yours,

FORRESTER B. WASHINGTON,
Supervisor of Negro Economics in Illinois.

HOW TO ESTABLISH AND CONDUCT A COOPERATIVE STORE.

How to start.—A store should not be started unless at least 100 members can be secured.

If sufficient interest is displayed, call a meeting to select a committee of five or seven to solicit subscribers, but accept no money until you have amount pledged sufficient to insure success.

Amount and value of stock.—According to the laws of Illinois no person can own and control more than five shares of the capital stock of such association. The shares of stock shall be not less than five dollars nor more than one hundred dollars a share. On account of the prevailing high prices, it has been found advisable to make the shares of stock not less than $10 a share. Not less than 50 per cent of the amount subscribed should be paid in at the time the organization of the store is completed.

Details.—As soon as a sufficient amount has been subscribed (not less than $2,500) call a meeting of all the subscribers and have them elect a board of directors for different periods of time, so that at least some will hold over. Do not elect anyone simply because he is a good fellow. Require whoever handles the funds to furnish a good bond.

No member should be allowed more than one vote, no matter what his shares or purchases.

Share and loan capital.—If a sufficient amount of share capital is not purchased, a store may secure loan capital from members interested in the success of the institution, whose share capital is paid in full, or the accumulated profits or earnings, usually called dividends to help finance the store after the share capital subscribed if fully paid.

Meeting of stockholders.—A meeting of stockholders should be held every three months. Special meetings may be called by the board of directors or by petition of the members.

Duties of board of directors.—The board of directors should meet once a week, pass upon and pay all bills, if correct, receive the report of the manager, and transact such other business that comes within their scope.

Location.—A good location is essential to success. A good building, not necessarily large, but in a good location, is much to be preferred, even at a higher rental.

Business management.—Stores should be conducted on a cash basis. Extending credit will ruin a store and the necessity of cash business should be impressed on the minds of all members.

Managers.—Next to the loyalty of the members, a good competent manager, an honest man, is the most important asset to a store. A technical education is not necessary, but a knowledge of business cooperation is. The manager should be given a great deal of discretion in the general supervision of the store. He should turn over to the treasurer or other authorized officer, at the close of each day's business, the day's receipts and a statement showing the amount of business for that day.

Employees.—So far as possible no immediate relative of the manager or a member of the board of directors should be employed in any capacity, as it creates jealousy and bad feeling.

Managers and clerks should be paid good wages as an incentive to do good work.

Buying a stock of goods.—Do not allow anyone to load your store up with an immense stock of goods that can not be turned over readily, as they will become shopworn and have to be sold later on at a loss. Goods should be turned over as often as possible, as the turnover is an essentially important feature in making money. All bills should be discounted and paid promptly. By no means should prices be cut and no manager should be allowed to undersell the surrounding stores. To do so invites trouble not only with your competitors, but wholesale houses as well.

Bookkeeping.—Lack of a good bookkeeping system has been the rock upon which many a cooperative store has been wrecked.

Banking.—All money taken in should be banked every day except the small amount that is kept on hand to take care of the cash business. All goods bought should be paid for by check. Care should be exercised not to have an overdraft at the bank.

Incorporation.—All stores should incorporate as a matter of protection.

Auditing accounts.—One of the most important features of a successful cooperative enterprise is a correct auditing system. The books and accounts of every store should be audited very carefully every three months, and wherever possible by an expert accountant.

Dividends.—Dividends in a cooperative store are paid, not on the investment as in a privately owned concern, but on the amount of purchases made by the shareholder.

At quarterly or semiannual periods, as may be determined on, a complete invoice should be taken, the profits ascertained, and after setting aside a substantial amount for a reserve fund (anywhere from 25 to 50 per cent of the profits) the balance should be paid in dividends on the basis of purchases during the period, or credited to them on their account,

Surplus earnings.—The term "dividends" as herein used is merely the accumulated savings or the surplus earnings of each member, which the society is under obligations to repay to the individual at a future date and should be distinguished from dividends as applied in the usual commercial transaction and in the future the cooperative movement should use the term "surplus earnings" instead of "dividends."

Further information.—Further information concerning the establishment and maintenance of cooperative stores can be obtained by writing to the Supervisor of Negro Economics for Illinois, 116 North Dearborn Street, Chicago, or to the Department of Agriculture, Washington, D. C., for Bulletin 394 on Cooperative Stores, price 10 cents, or to Duncan McDonald, secretary-treasurer, Central States Cooperative Society, Springfield, Ill,, who has issued a very interesting pamphlet on the subject, price 5 cents Butcher Workmen's Local 651, 4300 State Street, Chicago, has launched a cooperative store with all colored officers. They would be glad to give you the benefit of their experiences.

Although there were a number of activities in the State, the department was kept fully informed as to racial feeling in various localities in the State. Preceding the Chicago riots in July, 1919, regular information had been received through official channels concerning existing conditions. The riots brought sharply to the attention of the country an acute racial situation, the intensity of which had long been observed as developing in this district. Prior to July there had been sporadic clashes in one or two Illinois localities and the State supervisor had officially reported these outbursts. The Chicago Race Commission, as an outcome of this disturbance, gives strong promise of some constructive effort for preventing such difficulties in the future.

We may, then, summarize the activities and results in Illinois as follows:

1. *Conferences.*—State conferences in Illinois and Missouri resulting in exchange of facts and better understanding between representatives of Negro workers, white workers and white employers from a number of localities in the State, and the adoption of a plan of organization and program of work by means of which definite activities were undertaken throughout the territory. These activities resulted in better understanding and adjustment of relations between these three labor interests.

2. (*a*) *Surveys and information on Negro labor conditions.*—Surveys were made of 500 firms employing 50 or more Negroes, showing that approximately over 50 per cent reported their intention for retaining Negro help. The remaining 50 per cent were noncommittal; (*b*) The reports from 14 chairmen during the period of activity in Illinois, June, 1918, to July 1, 1919, indicated a growing scarcity of jobs for Negroes, with conditions most acute in Chicago.

3. *Board of managements.*—Constant advice and counsel were given to the United States Employment Service and the State employment service, and assistance was given to the board of management of the Soldiers and Sailors' Bureau and its branches.

4. *Publicity.*—(*a*) Fifteen articles in daily newspapers of Illinois for the purpose of stimulating interest in and employment of Negro workers; (*b*) 14 special articles for Negro press; (*c*) 10 addresses in public meetings; (*d*) magazine discussions of unemployment situation among colored women.

5. *Placements.*—Besides from the usual hundreds of placements shown in work of offices, a number of special opportunities were secured for specially qualified Negroes. These are cited on account of the usual difficulty in such instances.

6. *Volunteer work.*—(*a*) One thousand solicitations of firms over the telephone in the interest of returning colored soldiers; (*b*) 5,000 appeal letters to Chicago employers, 3 personal visits to Chicago employers; (*c*) organization and direction of "flying squadron" of returned soldiers to solicit positions for comrades.

7. *Returning colored soldiers.*—(*a*) Formation of board of management; (*b*) appointment of special solicitor; (*c*) shop addresses to a total of 17,000 Chicago employees on fair play in jobs for returning soldiers.

8. *Special investigations.*—(*a*) There were three special investigations involving unions, race relations, and discrimination matters; (*b*) investigation of industrial opportunities offered in other States, especially the southern States.

9. *Special conferences.*—(*a*) President Chicago Federation of Labor; (*b*) men of public works in Chicago; (*c*) State Advisory Board, United States Department of Labor, executive committee Soldiers' Bureau, Assistant Federal Director United-States Employment Service, superintendent Soldiers and Sailors' Bureau, chairman of board of management, representatives of churches, lodges, women's organizations.

10. *Cooperation.*—Cooperation was had through the supervisor of Negro economics and through local Negro workers' advisory committees with the following organizations: Y. M. C. A., Y. W. C. A., Chicago Urban League, Federation of Colored Women's Clubs, National Association for the Advancement of Colored People, American Federation of Labor, Chambers of Commerce, mayor of Cairo, aldermen of Chicago, superintendent of public schools, Springfield; city attorney of Cairo, State auditor of Jacksonville, and many other organizations and public officials.

11. *Miscellaneous.*—(*a*) Addresses to colored workers in industrial plants, emphasizing regularity, punctuality, and efficiency, etc.; (*b*) opportunities for colored college women; (*c*) opportunities for colored women in domestic work; (*d*) establishment of homes registration service.

CHAPTER XII.

REPORT OF WORK IN MICHIGAN.

Detroit, of course, is the great industrial center of Michigan, and to this point alone it was estimated that in the two years 1916–17 between 25,000 and 30,000 Negro migrants came. The department further estimated that these Detroit migrants came mainly from Alabama, Georgia, Florida, and Tennessee. Reasonable proportion of migrants in accordance with the calls of industry were, of course, distributed among other Michigan industrial cities, such as Kalamazoo, Benton Harbor, Flint, Grand Rapids, Saginaw, Port Huron, and other cities of equal or lesser importance in the industrial fabric of Michigan. The automobile industry made Detroit, necessarily, a most important point of destination for the Negro migrants.

The United States census recorded 5,741 Negro inhabitants of Detroit in 1910, while conservative estimates at the close of the war period placed the number at 35,000. Such an increase in Detroit and correspondingly in other Michigan cities created far-reaching problems of economics and made the State of Michigan essentially one where prompt endeavor on the part of the Department of Labor ought to be made. The Negro residential district of Detroit had become crowded, and as the Negro population spread it became difficult to secure houses in the various localities. Naturally, then, there came a tendency toward neighborhood segregation and a resulting sharp division between newcomers and the older residents. These conditions called for consideration and sympathy on the part of every agency, public or private, and in the mind of every person.

The pressing need of Michigan enterprises for laborers caused her industrial captains to make theretofore unheard-of wage conditions. Aside from the Negro laborer, thousands of workmen from all other parts of the country and from European cities soon found location in Michigan. Therefore the department sent a Negro expert to supervise and handle, cooperatively, the many problems growing out of the presence of an unusual number of Negro workers—skilled, semiskilled, and unskilled.

It seems pertinent to make a brief mention of some of the agencies which were functioning in economic and civic matters in Michigan cities prior to the establishment of the Division of Negro Economics.

The Michigan State labor department has always been well organized and had been giving its usual attention to purely local matters. The United States Employment Service of the Department of Labor had been well established in Michigan, and was growing rapidly in its power and capability to take the proper initiative in fostering and promoting the welfare of workers whenever such workers came under the supervision of the Government, particularly in regard to the war-labor program which included, in certain instances, beginning August 1, 1918, the recruiting and placing of large numbers of workers.

No arrangements had been made, however, by the United States Employment Service for handling the unusual problems which grew out of the presence of 30,000 or more Negro newcomers.   Among the private agencies which had been doing laudable work in the Detroit district there may be mentioned the Detroit Urban League, which had been successfully active and competent in handling the problems of Negro labor.   In this connection it is interesting to note some early experience which the Detroit Urban League had.

Number of male and female workers requested by employers through the joint employment office and the Detroit Urban League July 2 to Dec. 23, 1917.[1]

MALE.

Laborers	846	Metal carriers	16
Laborers (outside)	778	Tool makers	15
Truckers (automobile)	336	Repair vacuum cleaners	14
Janitors	225	Riveters	8
Molders	160	Metal (unspecified)	7
Machinists (unspecified)	109	Cutters (unspecified)	6
Porters (unspecified)	102	Watchmen	6
Laborers' helpers	69	Assembly men (automobile)	5
Yardmen	67	Assembly men's helpers	26
Kitchen men and dishwashers	54	Farm (unspecified)	3
Furnace tenders	70	Block testers	2
Mechanics	48	Pipe layers	2
Core makers	45	Rivet buckers	2
Housemen and bell boys	28	Paper hangers	2
Chauffeurs and crankmen	10	Miscellaneous (unspecified)	2,431
Elevator men	26		
Coal passers (laborers)	24	Total	5,542

FEMALE.

Laundry (day)	123	Factory (cigar)	18
Maids	45	Cook	15
Factory (garment)	32	Office	2
Dishwashers	24	Miscellaneous	14
General housework	25		
Ushers (theater)	19	Total	317

Number of Negro workmen employed on Apr. 27, 1917, by firms with which Detroit Urban League had touch.

Packard Motor Car Co. (May 18)	1,100	Detroit Pressed Steel Co	50
Buhl Malleable Iron Co	280	Hudson Motor Car Co	50
Ford Motor Car Co	200	Detroit Stove Works	27
Continental Motor Car Co	200	Paige Detroit Motor Car Co	20
Aluminum Castings Co	150	Saxon Motor Car Co	20
Michigan Steel Castings Co	170	Hupp Motor Car Co	20
Michigan Copper & Brass Co	125	Detroit Seamless Tubes Co	20
Michigan Central Railroad Co	100	Monarch Foundry	15
Michigan Malleable Iron Co	100	Michigan Smelting & Refining Co.	100
General Aluminum & Brass Co	65		
Chalmers Motor Car Co	62	Total	2,874

These data were compiled early in 1917 and therefore do not indicate the increase and pressing demand for Negro labor which existed at the climax of the war period.   They show, however, how the demand began to grow and how the inclusion of the Negro worker, in larger numbers than ever before, secured his economic standing in the great industry of Michigan.

---

[1] Reprinted from "Negro Newcomers of Detroit, Mich.," by George E. Haynes, Ph. D., published by Home Missions Council, New York City.

Such well-organized machinery for handling economic problems as was found in Michigan, lightened the plans of the department and called for a slightly different program from that which was to be followed in other States.

Forrester B. Washington, who, as is observed in the Illinois report, had been first appointed by the department as supervisor of Negro economics for Michigan, later, in June, 1918, began work, with headquarters at Detroit. Mr. Washington had been executive secretary of the Detroit Urban League and had handled personally more than 8,000 Negro workers during his earlier work in Detroit. In the following months of July, August, and September Mr. Washington formulated the early plans for the work of the Division of Negro Economics in Michigan. He made a number of surveys of labor in Michigan cities and, under the immediate supervision of the United States Employment Service, gave specific advice with regard to, and handled personally, a great number of Negro labor problems, particularly in the matter of recruiting. The early Michigan plans called for Negro workers advisory committee formations in the industrial district with a supervising State committee of white and colored persons.

Consequently the Michigan program was well formulated when, on October 1, 1918, Mr. Washington was transferred to Illinois, being succeeded in Michigan by Dr. William Jennifer, formerly special agent and examiner under the United States Employment Service with official station at Washington, D. C. Dr. Jennifer entered upon the work with a background of years of experience in matters relating to Negroes in the United States Bureau of the Census, where he had assisted in compiling the bulletin known as Negro Population in the United States 1790 to 1910. Dr. Jennifer took his post under the Michigan Federal director in October, taking up the plan as started by Mr. Washington.

Dr. Jennifer at once continued the seeking out of representatives of the industrial ranks, professional men, educators, and churchmen for increased cooperation in Michigan. His itinerary on this mission included Ypsilanti, Ann Arbor, Jackson, Battle Creek, Kalamazoo, Benton Harbor, Niles, Cassopolis, Grand Rapids, Saginaw, Bay City, Flint, Lansing, Port Huron, and Pontiac. Later, similar itineraries made possible his planning of the State conference for December 14, 1918. At that conference, which was presided over by the Federal director of the United States Employment Service, the committees on organization, plans of work, and women's work made their reports and an open discussion, in which all were invited to take a part, was had regarding the peculiar local problems of Michigan points. It was interesting to note that several special experiments were being made in Michigan respecting the efficiency of Negro women workers. This group of workers—in industry and in personal and domestic service—was of rather large proportions, hence the committee on women's work at the Michigan conference made a special report which follows.

EXTRACT OF REPORT OF COMMITTEE ON WOMEN'S WORK.

Plans devised for changing industries from a war basis to a peace basis, the main point being to bring about this change without throwing many out of employment.

1. See that the work is the proper sort of work for a woman or girl.

2. See that conditions are suitable—
    (*a*) From the hygienic standpoint.
    (*b*) From the moral standpoint.
3. Standards: Work to secure the following:
    (*a*) Eight-hour day.
    (*b*) Forty-five minutes lunch hour.
    (*c*) Ten minutes rest in the morning and 10 minutes in the afternoon.
    (*d*) No work between 10 p. m. and 6 a. m.
    (*e*) No sweatshop work.
4. Sanitary conditions (ventilation, lighting, temperature, cleanliness):
    (*a*) Such as affect washrooms, lunch rooms, lockers, toilets.
5. Minimize hazards connected with the work:
    (*a*) Such as result from fumes, dust, chemicals, dampness, and lack of proper ventilation.
    (*b*) Good environment.
    (*c*) Lifting not exceeding 25 pounds.
    (*d*) Wages—a living wage.
    (*e*) Age limit. (Conformation to child-labor laws.) (Education-compulsory laws.)
6. To further promote our plans, we must have a list of industries in which colored women are employed:
    (*a*) Investigate to find out cause where only white women are employed and strive to secure the employment also of colored women where such discrimination exists.
7. Efficiency should be striven for in several different ways:
    (*a*) Such as number of hours service given weekly.
    (*b*) Quality of service given.
    (*c*) Geniality of temperament, pleasing personality.
8. See if there be segregation in the rest rooms, and in the wages. If so, seek remedy:
    (*a*) See that in the training schools the colored girl gets the same advantage as the white girl.
    (*b*) See if there be a chance for promotion of colored girls in the factory or work-place under consideration.
    (*c*) Study the class of workers to which we make appeal.
    (*d*) Find out the attitude of the employer and employee each to the other. Strive for amicable adjustment of differences.
    (*e*) Study how the employer can be best appealed to and reached.

The undersigned committee accepts this outline as a basis for work and will organize to put it into operation in accordance with the needs of the individual localities.

Mrs. HELEN B. IRVIN, *Temporary Chairman.*
Mrs. E. C. HASKELL, *Secretary.*
Mrs. MAUD HENDERSON.
Mrs. E. L. JOHNSON.
Mrs. MARY E. McCOY.
Mrs. A. C. HAFFORD.
Mrs. MATTIE O. REED.
Mrs. MATTIE L. JOHNSON.
Mrs. Mrs. LUCY L. BERRY.
Mrs. HELEN B. BROWN.
Miss ETHEL HENSLEY.
Miss O. L. WILLIAMS.
Mr. JOHN M. RAGLAND.

Inasmuch as there already existed in the Department of Labor a women's bureau which was handllng, on a broad basis, policies respecting the ideals and accomplishments of women workers, the plans of this early Negro workers' conference were shaped to include the needs and conditions of women workers throughout the State. Out of the conference there grew a State Negro Workers' Advisory Committee, which was the overhead organization for the following county and city committees: Bay, Berrien, Genesee, Ingham, Jackson, Kalamazoo, Kent, Muskegon, Oakland, Saginaw, St. Clair, Washtenaw, Wayne, and Calhoun.

As illustative of the kind of cooperation which the department was able to secure in Michigan, the interests represented at the conference and on the State Negro Workers' Advisory Committee are cited as follows: The Y. W. C. A., the Y. M. C. A., the State Federation of Labor, the State Missionary Society, union and nonunion labor, merchants and business men, professional classes, the press, private and social welfare agencies and governmental agencies. All these units gave freely of their influence in the matter of shaping plans and policies for the welfare of Negro workers. Where there was such a community of interest industrial conditions and needs in the matter of racial adjustments were remedied with comparative ease, for reaching into any plan of solidarity of such a nature there come potential forces from every unit in the community and State and the ultimate successful results may be anticipated from the very beginning.

At later dates the Michigan supervisor visited practically every important point where Negro labor was involved throughout the State and the various county and city committees were given authority to carry forward concrete plans in labor matters. One or two strikes were investigated. The usual efforts in seeking and securing placements for Negro soldiers were made. Groups of laborers who were perhaps on the verge of striking were visited and conferred with, and their employers, where practicable, were given departmental advice. Congested housing conditions in Detroit and other cities were given such practical attention as were possible. Extraordinary efforts were made in seeking placements at plants for Negro women. A number of mass meetings for creating better sentiment and high morale were held at strategic points. In pressing cases of placements, telephone inquiries were made direct with Michigan factories and employment blanks and notices were given to men for filling out and filing. On Sundays it was possible to have read in Michigan churches notices of unusual interests to colored labor.

In Michigan, as in other States, there were found employers who had not employed colored workmen. Such employers were visited personally by the supervisor and were impressed with a statement of the efficiency, conduct, and work of many Negro workers in Michigan and elsewhere.

In all it would be difficult to tabulate specifically the many and varied steps which were taken in Michigan. Such steps, however, were based upon the complete plan of the Secretary of Labor and included the same policies that the Department of Labor was charged to carry out in the interests of all workers of the United States, white and colored, male or female.

The Federal director of the United States Employment Service commented with great favor upon the work of Dr. Jennifer, the Michigan supervisor of Negro economics. (See letter quoted on p. 23.)

CHAPTER XII.

REPORT OF WORK IN MISSISSIPPI.

Mississippi, with its great farm land and cotton areas, its tremendously active lumber interests, its thousands of Negro workers who were performing the greater part of labor in connection with those industries, offered many complex problems for the Department of Labor in carrying into this State the work of the Division of Negro Economics. From the strict standpoint of economics the output from the above industries had been jeopardized throughout the war period by the tremendously large migration northward by Negroes from the agricultural districts of Mississippi. It was difficult to estimate, as has been done in the other Southern States, the exact number of Negroes leaving Mississippi points, for the reason that a great many of them were drawn from between southern and northern Mississippi, while many others migrated to Arkansas regions and returned to Mississippi.

However, of the four to six hundred thousand Negroes who did in fact come from Southern States to the North during the war it is safe to say that Mississippi contributed a larger proportion than any other State in the South. On the part of workers it had long been alleged that Mississippi wages were low. Sawmill wages were quoted in 1916 as $1.10 a day, while ordinary hand labor in the agricultural districts, it is said, was paid for at rates as low as 60 and 75 cents a day. Four dollars a week was said to be a fair wage for domestic and personal service, and even though wages were reported to have increased during the period 1916-1918 from 10 to 25 per cent, northern industries drew from Mississippi thousands and thousands of its Negro workers, male and female. Being an agricultural State, producing cotton, foodstuffs, and the like, and Negro workers performing the bulk of labor in connection with agriculture, Mississippi labor shortage soon became a very serious matter to productivity of this State.

When the United States Employment Service with headquarters at Meridian, Miss., arranged to supervise the State work of the Division of Negro Economics, the racial consciousness of Negroes was so strongly developed and interracial relations became so cordial that it was possible at once to bring about an immediate cooperation of State, private, and Federal agencies which was not surpassed by that of any other State or locality. The State board of education, the Mississippi Welfare League, chambers of commerce throughout the State, the United States Department of Agriculture, the Mississippi Association of Teachers in Colored Schools, the Negro banks, colleges, and various other private organizations promptly pledged their full support to the work of Negro economics.

Consequently, following a preliminary trip through Mississippi of the Director of Negro Economics and following a meeting of the Southern Sociological Congress on July 12, 1918, the service of Negro economics was established under the immediate supervision of the

United States Employment Service, and Rev. J. C. Olden, who was well known and respected by citizens of Mississippi, was appointed as supervisor of Negro economics for that State. Prior to that time Mr. Olden had been assisting the United States Employment Service district superintendent in Mississippi and Alabama points in furthering the aims of the Employment Service and in stimulating the sentiment and desires of Negro workers. As a result, he had built up a strong chain of support, particularly in the churches and schools.

Among the early concrete results of the Negro workers' advisory committee there may be cited the three following:

1. Cooperation among the railroad shop workers of Meridian.

2. Discriminatory practices in connection with the "work card" system in Meridian were brought before the proper authorities and the entire scheme abolished.

3. The Federal director requisitioned the entire forces of our advisory committees and delegated to them the big responsibility of direct assistance in the placing of Negro soldiers.

It is apparent that these results were made possible through the new consciousness of the Negro wage earner as to his worth as a producing agent and as to his having a higher regard for his employer.

In November, 1918, the supervisor formulated a publicity program which was furthered throughout the State in January, 1919. The principal purposes of that program are given below, and it may be noted that through the county line-up of Negro workers' advisory committees in the State it was possible to reach every public and private school and college in the State as well as the public in general:

1. Members of advisory committee to present the work of the department before all schools in their respective districts where no travel is necessary.

2. Supervisor Negro economics to present the work before all schools and colleges not covered in this allotment. Allotments to be made and specific dates set at the meeting of State committee (December).

3. Each school and college will be asked to join the ranks and support the work and give a written indorsement of the same.

4. From time to time (afterwards) the schools will be kept in constant touch with our work by means of literature and personal visits.

5. The State department of education will be asked to indorse our program and release copies of their indorsement to all white superintendents and colored supervisors.

6. Assistant State supervisor of Negro schools will be asked to assist in allotting schools to committee members.

7. Members of the State committee will be urged to present our work before every public gathering—fraternal, business, religious—possible in their various districts.

8. All white organizations of influence that believe in the uplift of the Negro will be asked to indorse our program and lend every influence toward its accomplishment.

9. If possible the ministry of the State will be asked to prepare special sermons, bearing on our work, for the second Sunday in January.

10. Members of the State committee will be asked to see that in all emancipation celebrations for January 1 our work shall be presented.

As being concretely indicative of the record for the departmental work in Mississippi there may be mentioned the following typical commendations of two large Mississippi firms, which said:

1. We trust that you will remain in Meridian as long as you possibly can and make as many talks as it is possible for you to make to other employees as well as to ours.

2. We wish to write this testimonial unsolicited by you as to the beneficial results of your inspiring talks to our employees. We were very much impressed with your talks and found that our white employees seemed to enjoy them and profit by them as much as our numerous colored workmen.

The State Negro workers' advisory committee was effectively organized with a membership of 29 and having representation at the beginning from 25 counties of the State. Prompt steps were taken for the formation in the counties of subcommittees. Prof. R. S. Grossley, assistant supervisor of Negro schools, later field organizer for the United States Employment Service, made a survey of the northern portion of the State and outlined the organization of the county committees. The State committee decided that its plan of organization and work should be released to representatives of various welfare organizations of the State and that, as far as possible, the work should be outlined before local societies, such as the Red Cross, insurance companies, and the like. Letters stating the purpose and plans of the committee of organization were released through the United States Employment Service to its subsidiary officials throughout the State. Of interesting importance in the way of co-operation there should be mentioned the attitude of the Methodist Episcopal Conference of the State of Mississippi, which indorsed completely the departmental program. This conference had previously carried on a campaign in the interest of efficiency of Negro wage earners, and was quick to recognize the facility to be gained through official functions.

In January, 1919, the supervisor visited a number of Mississippi counties and cities, among which were McComb, Pike, Amite, Walthall, Lincoln, Marion, and Crystal Springs. At these points county teachers' meetings were attended and full cooperation of the teaching forces secured. Prof. Grossley, representing the State board of education, was present at these meetings and his subsequent work calls for the sincere thanks of the department to him and to the Mississippi State educational department for their constant help, Mr. Grossley having served throughout the work as a dollar-a-year man.

The domestic help problem mentioned previously in this report gained particular significance by March, 1919, and in line with the policies of the United States Employment Service to assist in relieving this problem a survey was made by the supervisor, from which the following facts were adduced:

1. Conditions.—(a) Unrest among domestic help; (b) constant shifting of domestic help; (c) lack of interest in work and efficiency among domestic help; (d) absolute refusal to work on part of domestic help.

2. Apparent causes.—(a) Low wages; (b) lack of sympathetic cooperation between women employers and women employees.

Concerning (c) and (d) under the conditions we find the following very human attitudes expressed in this simple manner:

What's the use of doing good work when we get poor pay? It is better to do nothing "for nothing" than to work "for nothing."

In the way of suggestions for relief the supervisor recommended that a vigorous campaign of conferences with women workers be begun, together with added assistance from the colored ministry to the end that cooperation of the women workers and women employers might bring forth some concession on the part of employers to the efficient women workers in the matter of wages. These conferences were had and, in many instances, the problem was much relieved.

The program of work of Negro workers' advisory committees varied to some extent in accordance with the peculiar conditions of each State. The program of work which was outlined for Mississippi is given below as showing the most stable means of accomplishing the objects of the work in this State.

1. *Calling together colored representatives.*—It will probably be well to call together four or five most responsible colored citizens (at least one of them should be a woman) in your county, town, or city and go over with them in detail, the plans and purpose of the State Negro workers' advisory committee. In calling together these persons all possible factionalism should be avoided. The men and women called together should be the leaders of various organizations and the various occupations of the community.

2. *Get in touch with white employers.*—The Federal Director of the United States Employment Service of your State, or the Supervisor of Negro Economics will give you, if you write him, the names of some white citizens of your community whom these officials depend upon for local matters. You also know some of the most responsible and trusted white employers of your locality. It will be well to go to them for information and advice about cooperation of white people in your efforts on labor questions affecting the colored people. In case you do not know the name and address of the State official, write for the information to the chairman of your State Negro workers' advisory committee or to Dr. George E. Haynes, Director of Negro Economics, Department of Labor, Washington, D. C.

3. *Explain to white citizens the organization of the State committee.*—The representative white men in your community should be interested. Get in touch with two or three of them, as suggested under No. 2, and tell them about the organization of the State Negro workers' advisory committee. Explain to them that this committee has cooperative white members; explain further the plan to have a county and neighborhood Negro advisory committee with white cooperative members. It is well to ask their help in securing white citizens as permanent cooperating members of the county and local advisory committees. As soon as you decide on representative colored men for members of your local committee, and white men who may be recommended for cooperating members, send those names, with comments about the persons, their occupations and other connections, to the chairman of your State advisory committee.

4. *Reaching the colored population.*—The large numbers of colored people may be reached through the churches and the lodges. A personal visit made by you or some other responsible person to talk to those attending each church and each lodge is necessary. They need to be informed about the relation of their productive labor to agriculture and industry. It will help also to secure white citizens to talk to Negro audiences. The facts about the purpose of the Department of Labor in organizing these Negro workers' advisory committees should be stated (see Article II of the constitution of the committee). Explain the present labor crisis and the important part Negroes are playing and can play in getting one hundred per cent production. The Department of Labor desires to get these constructive plans before your community very soon by your help and the help of others on the State Committee. As soon as you are in a position to put further plans in operation, please signify that by writing the chairman of your State Advisory Committee or to the Supervisor of Negro Economics, Department of Labor, Meridian, Miss.

5. *Cooperation in adjusting conditions.*—If there is anything in your community which is causing restlessness and dissatisfaction among the colored people and you think these should be brought to the attention of white employers go to two or three white citizens whom you can trust or the cooperating members of your committee and ask them to help you get the facts relating to such dissatisfaction before the members of local authorities or employers.

Please bear in mind, however, especially in giving complaints, by all means to have some constructive plans and suggestions to correct and satisfy the complaints of the colored people. As you will agree, it is not sufficient and it is poor policy to go forward at any time with complaints and not have positive plans for remedying them. Some practical, constructive suggestions and plans which can be proposed to remedy causes are by all means essential.

Furthermore, we should not always expect to have our plans to remedy those conditions adopted. Other citizens may have better plans. The aim of the Negro workers' advisory committees is to help with constructive plans and programs to assist our country in getting the largest production in agriculture and industry and at the same time to help secure improved conditions among Negro wage earners. Both these ends can best be reached by constructive plans and programs.

6. There is being organized, now, by the United States Employment Service what are known as community labor boards, made up of representatives of the employers, of the employees, and of the United States Employment Service. You should get in touch with the white men who are on your local community labor board. If there

is no local board, you should endeavor to obtain, through the Supervisor of Negro Economics, the names of white citizens with whom you should get in touch on employment matters.

In case you do not know who the local members of your community labor board are, you should write to the Federal Director of the United States Employment Service of your State, to your State Supervisor of Negro Economics, or to the Department of Labor, Washington, D. C.

7. *Some of the types of work which you can begin.*—(*a*) Holding public mass meetings to inform the people about the need for systematic labor; (*b*) Discussions at regular church and lodge meetings and other gatherings; (*c*) Bringing to the attention of the United States Employment Service any misunderstandings among the colored people about the use of that service by them.

Further suggestions will be furnished you upon request.

Any other things which it seems to you it would be well to do in your community you may take up with the chairman of your State Advisory Committee or with the Supervisor of Negro Economics of your State, if one has been appointed.

GEORGE E. HAYNES,
Director of Negro Economics.

OCTOBER, 1918.

January, 1919, found the work in Mississippi well under way. The program of work had been presented at the Meridian Emancipation celebration exercises. The introductory card made up by the supervisor and approved by the Federal director to be used in connection with the recruiting had been sent out and a subsequent State committee meeting, as the work developed, had been planned. This meeting was held on January 27, 1919, in the Board of Trade Building of Jackson, Miss., and the following points were discussed:

1. Organization.
2. Efficiency of Negro labor.
3. Better conditions for farm labor.
4. Boys Working Reserve.
5. Plantation life in the Delta.

The Federal Director of the United States Employment Service was present and emphasized the need for a readjustment between men, races, and nations, and the common basis of understanding of right and justice. A cordial spirit of good will and hearty cooperation existed throughout the meeting and every interest was more strongly linked up than ever before in the purpose of furthering the plans of the Department of Labor. The organization of the Boys Working Reserve, an organization of youthful members to substitute for men who were in the Army in planting and harvesting the agricultural crops, was taken up. Later on the Boys Working Reserve Organization among Negro youth of Mississippi became efficient and helpful. At the close of January the plans as applicable to Mississippi were well established for returning soldiers. In February 1919 the Supervisor visited Yazoo City, Greenwood, Indianola, Greenville and Vicksburg. He reported increased thrift among Negro men and women and full time labor in the cotton fields. He reported, however, that in regions where conditions were particularly bad there were miles and miles of fields of unpicked cotton.

In December, 1918, Supervisor Olden, who returned to his ministry, was succeeded by Lemuel L. Foster, who took over the duties as supervisor of Negro economics for Mississippi. Mr. Foster had been trained at Fisk University, had done considerable welfare and social work in the South, and for one month prior to his appointment, had given voluntary assistance to the United States Employment Service in furthering its work. Mr. Foster took up with vigor the program begun by his predecessor and supervised the work until its close, June 30, 1918. Among the surveys he made a special report on two of the large lumber companies of Mississippi, which had realized the need of uniformly good working conditions and recreational facilities for its workers. He reported in these two instances a contented and efficient working force and a lack of turnover. These surveys were considered of sufficient importance for a departmental release and the facts were given wide publicity in order to stimulate other employers and other employees, respectively, to establish and to hope to receive the same treatment.

The membership on the advisory committee of white and colored citizens included the former mayor of Meridian, the vice president of the Citizens' National Bank, the clerk of the chancery court, and a prominent business man, all of whom were representative white citizens, shows again the type of cooperation which the department was able to secure. (For letter commending the work, see p. 23.)

CHAPTER XIII.

REPORT OF WORK IN NEW JERSEY.

Prior to the war, Negro workers had been employed here and there in industrial and agricultural pursuits in New Jersey. A fairly good wage was paid to the Negro workers in the occupations to which they were admitted. With the increased demands of the war, industries in New Jersey quite naturally became attractive locations for thousands of Negroes who came north. It is estimated that at least 25,000 Negro migrants located in the cities of New Jersey during the period of 1916–17. The probable distribution of these newcomers, on the estimated basis, is indicated in the following table:

New York Central camp, Weehawken	500
Erie camps:	
Weehawken	300
Jersey City	100
Philadelphia & Reading, Pennsylvania R. R., etc., camps	1,300
Jersey City	3,000
Newark	7,000
Carneys Point	3,500
Trenton	3,000
Camden	2,000
Bayonne, Paterson, and Perth Amboy	4,000
Wrightstown and South Jersey	3,000
Orange, Montclair, Paterson	3,000
Total	30,700

Various agencies, Federal, State, and private, were keeping in touch with conditions affecting the labor situation of New Jersey for some time prior to the establishment of the Division of Negro Economics. Among the more important agencies giving special attention to Negro affairs were the Associated Charities of Newark, the Urban League of Newark, and the State Bureau of Negro Migrants of the State Department of Labor, under the direction of Col. Lewis Bryant. This work caused increased attention to be given to matters pertaining to Negro workers. Correlating the efforts of these organizations, the United States Employment Service had carried forward the employment policies and developed the recruiting and placement facilities in every field of labor, including Negro labor. It was quite natural, then, that the Department of Labor, having established a special Negro economics service, should turn to these agencies in the beginning for advice and assistance in putting into effect its special plans for improving conditions and relations of Negro workers.

A hasty preliminary survey was undertaken in Newark, N. J., by William M. Ashby, at that time executive secretary of the Urban League, at Newark, N. J., and later supervisor of Negro economics for New Jersey. The city of Newark was the largest industrial center in the State and was a pivotal point from which departmental activities affecting Negro workers might be well directed.

88

The Negro population in Newark in 1910 was approximately 10,000. By 1918 there had been an addition of from 8,000 to 10,000 and at the close of 1918 this number had been increased. The mean number of deaths for 1917 was about 550, or probably 20.23 per cent per 1,000, a rather large number, probably on account of the newcomers from the South who were subjected to very unfavorable housing and living conditions under the severe New Jersey climate, and who were not advised as to proper clothing. These figures were corroborated by prominent insurance companies.

Unlike most cities, in Newark there had been previously no distinct Negro quarters. With the influx of newcomers, however, Negro districts formed and from a few families large neighborhoods developed. The general trend of living conditions indicated a merging together of the older residents and the newer Negro population. Housing conditions were poor and rents were high. In a number of cases 10 and 12 persons lived in two or three rooms. The high purchase prices of properties and excessive rents, which increased in keeping with the law of demand and supply, and the restricted area where colored people could purchase, often keep the newcomers from securing suitable quarters.

Negroes were engaged, principally, in the unskilled work in chemical plants, transportation, trucking, shipyard work, leather factories, iron molding, foundries, construction, and team driving. In Newark the Negro construction workers and iron shipbuilding workers formed a union which did not win the recognition of the secretary of the State Federation of Labor because he said the Negroes wanted to choose a name that was already in use by another union. A smeltermen's union was organized in Trenton among the Negroes. Their delegate sits in the Federated Union Council of the city. A hod carriers' union, Local No. 1, elected a Negro as delegate. This union has about 1,200 members, about 50 per cent of whom are white. The teamsters' union of whites and Negroes has a Negro delegate.

It is estimated that 6,000 male and 1,000 female workers were employed in the several industries in Newark alone. The Negro female workers found employment in toy factories, shirt factories, clothing factories, and glue factories, at an average wage of about $8 a week. In the shell-loading plants the pay was much higher. This is true of pieceworkers in other occupations, too. Negro women were also at work in garment factories, tobacco factories, toy factories, shell-loading plants, celluloid manufacturing, food production, leather-bag making and trunk making, as well as in assorting cores in foundries.

Negro women became reluctant to take positions as domestic servants on account of increasing demands for their services in industrial plants. Occasionally, a machinist, a carpenter, a millwright found employment as a skilled worker, and hundreds of riveters were employed in the Federal shipbuilding agencies and districts, not to speak of private concerns. Calkers and shipfitters were also in demand. Anglesmiths, boiler makers, packers, molders, steel chippers, and stationary firemen found ample employment.

As a hopeful sign there may be pointed out the small amount of friction between male workers of the two races; race relations were scarcely ever other than harmonious. Difficulties were more frequent among females. There were difficulties, also, when Negro skilled workers were first put on any job. Also, there were occasional difficulties where white and colored workers were engaged in the same plant.

The Negro church is the most effective agency for dealing with Negro workers, and through their church life a larger connection can be made than in any other way, but, unfortunately, it was only the individual ministers who took the Negro's industrial advantage seriously and tried to point out to him the industrial virtues. The church situation, therefore, is always an important factor to understand in any community. Newark is predominantly a Negro Baptist community. In some cases, migrants from the South brought pastors of their own denominations with them and they reestablished their congregations in the new home. The department found a great need for handling social and industrial problems and began cautiously to develop a program of work for the entire State.

Accordingly, William M. Ashby, mentioned above, a graduate of Lincoln and Yale Universities and a man of unusual experience in industrial and social work, was released by his organization to the Department of Labor to be supervisor of Negro economics for New Jersey. Mr. Ashby at once made a brief investigation of certain New Jersey firms, visiting the cities of Elizabeth, Jersey City, Bayonne, Garwood, Mays Landing, Camden, Paterson, Camp Dix, Camp Merritt, Atlantic City, Carneys Point, and other strategic points. Prominent firms in these cities, engaged in fulfilling both Government contracts and contracts for private firms and individuals, expressed their desire for the assistance of the Department of Labor.

To three large firms in Camden the supervisor suggested the placement of a Negro foreman, in order to handle with the greatest satisfaction gangs of Negro workers. This suggestion was adopted in each case. At Amatol, a shell-loading plant was approached by the supervisor on the matter of the diversion of a large number of colored women workers from Atlantic City. Three hundred and eighty-five such workers were secured in a few days.

A large plant at Paulsboro, which was running only one-fourth of its capacity on account of the labor shortage, was assisted by recruiting workers from Camden. This firm was engaged in making French shells. At Camden, a shipbuilding company received a supply of Negro workers through the employment activity of the supervisor.

For a firm in Garwood, which was making steel and brass rods for the United States Navy, men were recruited from Newark. To a Jersey City firm with a Government contract to supply meat for overseas, the supervisor brought, within five days, about 45 Negro workers. At Pompton Lakes, a plant running only to about 60 per cent of its capacity because of labor shortage was assisted in securing about 25 colored men. This plant had feared racial friction; but under the advice of the supervisor, no racial trouble came as a result of bringing these colored men.

In Grasseli, Newark, Edgewater, Kearney, Lakehurst, Freehold, Chrome, and Bound Brook, at later dates, the supervisor gave similar assistance, placing in all over 250 Negro workers in the course of about three weeks.

On another itinerary, the supervisor visited Paterson, Elizabeth, Orange, Plainfield, Bayonne, Trenton, Atlantic City, Asbury Park,

Perth Amboy, Dover, and Roebling, making observations of labor shortages and assisting in recruiting and placing Negro workers to supply the needs.

As samples of such observations and practical action which followed, there are cited below five brief investigations conducted by the New Jersey supervisor in November, 1918:

1. A female employee of the ——— Co., being an operator on a night shift, was overheard by me to complain of unjust treatment on a threat of ejection in the middle of the night from the plant of the aforesaid company, by one of its assistant foremen. Fearing that her story, though harmlessly told, would create an erroneous impression and probably thereby menace the opportunity of other operatives, I interrupted her and asked her to repeat it to me. Upon hearing it in full, I took her to the representative of the company in this office and with her assistance an interview with the employment manager and general manager was secured. The statement of her case in this interview—at which also was the assistant foreman against whom the complaint was made—was thoroughly considered and satisfactorily settled. Thus, the suspicions of other Negro workers who were sought for this plant were met and dispelled.

2. In an attempt to produce greater efficiency among the colored women operatives of the ——— Co., I had a lady of our department, along with the lady in charge of a colored social settlement, interview the superintendent of the women's department of the company. The superintendent of the above-mentioned company reports that, as against 12 colored women, the number with which they started three months ago, there are now 122 colored women, and that their work is very creditable under the direction of a matron who is colored. Efficiency clubs will be organized in this shop.

3. A female employee of the ——— Co. complained of discrimination received at the plant for which she worked. The supervisor of Negro economics had the matter investigated and received report that this company had ceased operation on account of cancellation of contract. Case can not be carried further.

4. A general circular form was sent to 55 employers of Negro labor throughout the State of New Jersey, to ascertain the quality of the work which is being given by such labor. The replies are varied, the general tone being very commendable.

5. The investigation at the ——— plant revealed that there are now about 60 colored women operatives whose work is commendable as against the unit of 10 which we started there when the opportunity was opened.

In keeping with the plans of the department, the New Jersey conference, drawn along the lines of prior conferences in other States, was called and held on Friday, November 22, 1918. Representative citizens, white and colored, from all over the State were present. The following program was carried out:

The constitution of the Negro workers' advisory committee was adopted, and shortly thereafter the formation of committees was begun. On account of the location of persons and problems in the cities of New Jersey, it was more practicable to begin at first the formation of the city committees than to follow the plans of other States and form, first, the State and county committees. Accordingly Negro workers' advisory committees were soon formed in Paterson, Newark, Camden, Trenton, Atlantic City, and several other New Jersey points. These committees functioned under the direction of the State supervisor of Negro economics and in close cooperation with the United States Employment Service and other public and private organizations.

As a sample of other activities in this State, the following extracts are given. The following concerns the peculiar condition which the New Jersey supervisor found at Camp Dix, N. J.:

REPORT ON SITUATION AMONG COLORED SOLDIERS AT CAMP DIX, N. J., WHO ARE TO
BE DEMOBILIZED SOON.

On Friday, January 3, 1919, I went to Camp Dix. Immediately on my arrival I went to Y. M. C. A. Hut No. 7, which is used by Negro soldiers. Mr. Shelby Davidson, secretary, and Mr. C. T. Greene, assistant secretary, were interviewed. In the course of interview the point of most significance was the fact that there was a decided aversion on the part of all the men attaching their names to anything which spelled United States, as most of them believed it meant reenlistment. This corroborated the statement made by Mr. William Banks, of the Employment Service, now in the camp. The secretary mentioned also the fact that men from the United States Employment Service had talked to the colored men to enlist their interest, but few had gone over.

I then went to Building 928, where I met Col. Casper H. Cole, the commandant, and Mr. William Banks, who is in charge of the United States Employment Service in the camp. I inquired whether colored men came into the office in great numbers. The answer was negative. The reason for this was, I believe, due to what was said above, that men are afraid to sign their names to Government matters. I asked if the command that all soldiers in the camp be marched to the employment office before their demobilization applied to colored as well as white men. The answer was affirmative.

After their supper I spoke to about 300 colored men in the Y. M. C. A. and explained the situation more clearly relative to the Government's position in interest of getting men work as soon as they are discharged.

My suggestion on the situation as applicable to all men in the camp, white and colored alike, is that in speaking of railroad opportunities men say "Pennsylvania Railroad," "Reading Railroad," or "Santa Fe," etc., instead of saying United States Railroad Administration, and also that in speaking of shipyards they say "Submarine," "Newport News," "Bristol," "Tampa," etc., instead of United States Shipping Board. This would eliminate from the minds of men the idea of a connection between the idea of a job and the Government.

WILLIAM M. ASHBY,
Supervisor of Negro Economics for New Jersey.

The following letter shows the type of effort inaugurated during the reconstruction period to give first-hand assistance through the United States Employment Service to returning soldiers:

Circular letter of advice.

MARCH 27, 1919.

From: The Director of Negro Economics.
To: The Supervisors of Negro Economics.
Subject: Cooperation with War Camp Community Service.

1. I find that the War Camp Community Service has a number of camps for Negro soldiers and sailors, and I am informed that it is cooperating with the United States Employment Service. I have talked with some of the representatives about their colored work and have also taken up the matter with the Director General, United States Employment Service, and the National Director of the Bureau for Placing Returning Soldiers and Sailors. It is agreeable to the national director for you to take up with the Federal director of the employment service of your State the question of utilizing such of these war camps as seem suitable for assisting in placing Negro soldiers and sailors.

2. You will find inclosed a list of the communities where there are activities for colored soldiers, together with the names of the workers. I advise that you take this up with the Federal director and assist him in getting in touch with such of these people as he wishes to.

Respectfully,

GEORGE E. HAYNES,
Director of Negro Economics.

Approved:
EDWARD EASTON, Jr.,
National Superintendent,
Bureau for Returning Soldiers and Sailors.
WADE H. SKINNER,
Acting Director, Organization Division,
U. S. Employment Service.

Some sample replies to letters of the New Jersey Supervisor contain statements regarding the employment of Negro workers. These responses were in reply to a questionnaire the object of which was to secure the information:

With reference to the questionnaire received from you, we are pleased to advise that we are using Negro workers as porters, elevator operators, matrons, dishwashers, and for other miscellaneous positions in the restaurant.

During the war we engaged quite a number of colored women to act as elevator operators. In all branches of the work, we have found Negro workers entirely satisfactory.

———

Answering your favor of recent date with reference to the Negro workers in our plant, I beg to state that we are well pleased with their work and I find them to be good and willing workers under the supervision of our white foremen, whom we have instructed to give every colored man or woman applying for work to this company the most cordial treatment, not the variety that will antagonize and drive them away from the job.

My personal dealings in the past as Employment and Welfare Manager, with the white and Negro workers have proven successful, as I have found that through kindness and friendly treatment, eliminating all profanity and personal insults, the majority of the Negro workers will do the work assigned to them thoroughly and to any company's satisfaction.

At present we have in our employ several hundred Negroes employed as general factory helpers only, but in the near future I hope to be successful in inducing my company to employ Negro mechanics. * * *

———

Answering your inquiry of the 4th inst., would advise that about 40 per cent of our labor is Negro. We do not find them to be as steady workers as the whites, although, in some instances, they have proven to be very faithful.

We use them largely on work where muscular strength and endurance are of prime importance and in this they work out quite well.

In a very few instances we have them operating machines, and, although we consider these workers above the average, their work is very satisfactory.

———

Your letter, requesting information regarding our colored employees, was received.

We have, altogether, about 1,250 colored men and 6 women. Of the latter, 4 are in our main restaurant as dishwashers, and two in our administration buildings, who keep the ladies' room in order. As a general rule our Negro workers give satisfaction. Almost all of them are employed on the ships. They seem to make very good riveters, bolters-up and chippers and caulkers. Those who recently came from the South seem to feel the cold weather, but the others who are acclimated, are as strong and hardy as the white men.

Among the number we have there are about 75 or 100 West Indian Negroes. There are no colored men doing clerical work here at all. There are some working as laborers, and as far as I know none are in the machine shops.

The following statements of Mr. Ashby, the New Jersey supervisor of Negro economics, give a very full insight into certain of his activities. These reports cover various periods following the signing of the armistice and show the complete turning over of departmental machinery to meet peace-time demands in the industrial life of the State:

I am very pleased to report a slight change for the better on the New Jersey conditions of Negro labor this week. At the opening of the past week the offices found themselves unable to make opportunities but later in the week new developments occurred. This was true, particularly, of Newark where about 125 men were referred during the week, at least 90 per cent of whom were placed. These openings were made possible largely because of personal solicitation upon two industries. * * *

The unemployment situation is particularly acute in Jersey City now.   The same is true of Camden.   In the former it is temporary, due to the strike of the Marine workers in and about the port of New York.   Many Negroes are stevedores on both the New York and New Jersey sides and due to the fact that transportation is tied up their work is made impossible.   In Camden, however, the lack of plants running on full time and also the crowding in of applicants from Philadelphia make it difficult to do much placing.

———

The great problem with which I am most concerned at the present, is that of the returning soldiers. Many commissioned officers and also many men who distinguished themselves in the Fifteenth and Buffalo regiments are New Jersey men. An appreciable number of these fellows are especially well prepared. I mention two or three—an illustrator and pen and pencil etcher, really talented; a tractor operator, graduate of the Scientific Course at Rutgers College; an auditor, near completion of his course in the New York School of Finance.   For the tractor operator, I have made, I believe, a position; but the remaining two are unemployed and it is rather criminal to offer to such men the most ordinary opportunities we have.

CHAPTER XIV.

REPORT OF WORK IN NEW YORK.

Owing to special complications in the New York situation no State conference was held. There was such delay in getting the situation in hand that the supervisor of Negro economics, Mr. Jesse O. Thomas, did not enter upon duty until September, 1918, just two months before the signing of the armistice, and his services were discontinued because of lack of funds after the end of that fiscal year. A New York Negro Workers' Advisory Committee was proposed in cooperation with the United States Employment Service and the New York City Employment Service and with the supervising commissioner of the New York State Industrial Commission, but this committee did not get fully to work before the readjustment came in the finance and plans of the United States Employment Service, under which the activities were carried on. A branch office of the United States Employment Service was opened in the Harlem district jointly with the State bureau of employment of the State industrial commission, under Supt. Prince L. Edwards, and supervision given to this from October, 1918, to March, 1919, and much work was done in meeting the difficult problems of placing semiskilled and skilled Negro workers in industrial establishments in New York City and vicinity. A large number of these men where returned Negro soldiers. The Submarine Boat Corporation may be mentioned, particularly, as having taken into employment a number of men of technical training and experience. Large numbers of the returning Negro soldiers, both New York residents and those from other places, called for special service from the placement agencies developed by the Federal Government and the State employment department. The supervisor of Negro economics for New York gave special help in the development of this work. A survey was made of labor conditions in Buffalo, N. Y., in April, 1919, showing considerable unemployment because of the closing down of munition plants and because of the military demobilization returning many men from overseas. Unskilled Negro labor, however, could be placed without very much difficulty, but semiskilled and skilled Negro workmen here, as in other places in the State, found great difficulty in finding employment. Very few industrial plants in the city employed colored women. Some of the firms, although employing thousands of workers, employed no colored or only a few, and these only in the menial occupations such as maids porters, janitors, or unskilled laborers. Similar surveys were made in Rochester, Albany, and New York City and environs. Both in New York City, Buffalo, and other parts of the State the Negro service of the department was heartily received by both white and colored citizens, but only got well started before curtailment of appropriations made it necessary to discontinue its preparations.

Investigations were made of charges of discrimination against colored workers and steps taken, in each case where the facts warranted, to remove the handicap. When the housing situation began to be acute the supervisor made a survey of important cities of the State to ascertain the exact condition as it related to the Negro wage earners with the view to assisting the United States Homes Registration Service in developing home-finding facilities, if thought advisable.

Among the many organizations giving active cooperation special mention should be made of the National Association of Colored Women and its president, Mrs. Talbert, whose particular activity was in the field at Buffalo, N. Y., and Mrs. Annette W. Erdmann, of the industrial committee of the New York City Urban League, whose untiring effort and hearty zeal were largely responsible for getting such results as were possible under the complicated difficulties and conditions.

CHAPTER XV.

REPORT OF WORK IN NORTH CAROLINA.

North Carolina was selected as the State in which the initial effort of the Department of Labor should be made, and its program established for promoting and fostering the welfare of Negro wage earners through the special service of Negro economics. Consequently, following an official trip of the Director of Negro Economics into important points in the State a conference of representative white and colored citizens was called by Hon. T. W. Bickett, governor of North Carolina, on June 19, 1918. There were present at this conference, which was held in the office of the governor, 17 of the most substantial Negro citizens from all parts of the State and five white citizens, as described in Chapter II. At the close of the meeting the governor appointed a temporary committee which drafted a constitution provided for the Negro Workers Advisory Committee, and for an organization of local county and city committees. The working plan of organization, with slight modifications and adjustments, which served as a model for the development of voluntary field organizations in other States, has been previously explained in the description of activities in other States.

Before discussing the subsequent steps of organization and activity in North Carolina, brief attention is here given to a few general and specific industrial and agricultural situations which obtained in North Carolina.

These situations are cited for the purpose of showing the wide scope of the field of Negro work into which the policies and plans of the Division of Negro Economics were to be carried.

The chief occupations of Negro women were in the field of agriculture, laundry work, domestic service, some work in spinning mills (and some in hosiery and underwear), and work in tobacco factories. There was a scarcity of female labor and on that account a number of silk mills had been closed. The cotton-mill season extends from May to September, and the tobacco season from September to April. In many instances the homes of workers were of a poor type; the streets and sidewalks fronting such homes were unpaved and poorly lighted. Surface drainage existed and general sanitation was inadequate in some cases. On the other hand, there were large numbers of well-cared-for homes in communities of intelligent and progressive Negroes.

In one North Carolina city it was reported that a Negro union had been organized to which the white workers objected. At New Bern, lumber industries employing large numbers of Negroes were reported as having "working conditions which were unpleasant." At Wilmington Negroes were employed in the shipyards, but only in the unskilled occupations. At various other points in North Carolina Negroes found employment in tanneries, hosiery mills, guano plants, box factories, and the like Throughout the State there were found a number of physicians, dentists, druggists, and a more than usual ownership of store and office buildings. At Kingston 5,000 Negro women and children were reported working in tobacco factories. At Waynesville there were found mill girls, garment workers, and a few clerks, organized and unorganized. As a general situation throughout the State, Negro labor was much in demand and was affected by the usual factors—(a) the union, (b) low wages, (c) housing conditions, (d) health, (e) opportunity for advancement, (f) the general competition between white and colored workers.

Following the conference the plan for cooperation and for the subsequent formation and activity of a State committee and subsidiary county and city committees was perfected. Among the early agencies of cooperation may be mentioned the United States Public Reserve, the State department of education, the rank and file of Negro colleges and universities in North Carolina, chambers of commerce and the Negro private organizations, including the church. An initial State committee of 29 substantial Negro citizens from various sections of the State was formed. The membership of the State committee and its executive board represent the following cities: Winston-Salem, Wadesboro, Winton, Oxford, Charlotte, Henderson, Raleigh, Greensboro, Rocky Mount, Tarboro, Salisbury, Chadbourn, New Bern, Lumberton, Bricks, Lexington, Durham, Method, Goldsboro, Wilmington, Wilson, and Asheville, thus bringing into play the influence and forces of the best citizens throughout the State. This committee was supplemented by interested white citizens, who became cooperating members.

This State committee and the subsidiary county committee, after adopting the constitution, started out in their activities under the supervision of Dr. A. M. Moore, who was appointed Supervisor of Negro Economics and special agent of the United States Employment Service. It should be stated that Dr. Moore served the department throughout the entire period of the war and the following seven months as a dollar-a-year man.

The early formation of county and city committees included the following counties: Guilford, Craven, Vance, Rockingham, Buncombe, Granville, Forsyth, Beaufort, Durham, Hertford, Alamance, and Edgecombe, Halifax, and Nash combined. When the work was closed on June 30, 1919, names had been submitted covering practically every county in the State.

Inasmuch as the Division of Negro Economics was in the immediate office of the Secretary of Labor, who was also chief administrative officer for the United States Employment Service as well as all the other departmental bureaus and divisions, it was practicable that the North Carolina Negro work, as did the work in other States, should have a close relationship to the United States Employment Service in that State. Consequently under the plan of organization for the State, the Federal Director of the United States Employment Service became an advisory member of the State Negro Workers' Advisory Committee. Also a close relationship with the governor, the chairman of the State Council of Defense, and other white men acting as advisers to other committees, was perfected and the following initial recommendation for North Carolina was gradually worked out and approved

1. Workers appointed for special activities among Negro wage earners will work under the authority of the United States Employment Service to give them official standing, with cooperation and supervision of the Federal State director.

2. The work shall be undertaken with the advice of the Director of Negro Economics.

3. Matters calling for the expenditure of funds shall be submitted with the approval of the Federal director and with the advice of the Director of Negro Economics.

4. All work carried on which relates to the Employment Service shall be undertaken with the approval of the Federal State director.

These plans of course were "overhead" plans, but they covered the many details which became properly applicable to local committees in the State as they were found. In order to bring the plans to the attention of the public the special agent succeeded in getting in close touch with the white and Negro members throughout the State, and in making arrangements for a publicity service which would not conflict with the Information and Education Service of the department.

Among some of the earlier problems were found (1) that many North Carolina laborers had been recruited through employment agencies and in an indiscriminating way many of the "shiftless" and "unstable" had been imported into North Carolina cities; (2) no particular opportunity had been offered to thrifty, dependable workmen to buy homes and to become permanent residents of the State. In subsequent plans of publicity and contact these two problems were dealt with by the North Carolina special agent and the close of the work found at each particular point but a few scattered persons who might be designated "shiftless."

The Supervisor of Negro Economics, having business interests of his own, soon found it necessary to have an assistant who could actively canvass cities throughout the State. Mr. R. McCants Andrews was subsequently detailed for such assistance work. Of the early problems which he faced there came report of race friction in a city of eastern North Carolina at a point in which there were members of the Negro workers' advisory committees. An investigation was made as to the nature of such race friction and valuable advice was given both to the employing class and to the working class, which resulted in removal of racial friction. In this connection valuable assistance in the matter of sentiment was given by a leading North Carolina paper, to the attention of which was called the value of mediation between white workers, white employers and Negro workers followed by a spirit of conciliation and cooperation and the abilty to see both sides of any issue. It was pointed out also that the common interest of the white employer who wants to engage the service which the Negro wage earner has to offer will make the adjustment of the labor situation a most important one. This paper gave publicity not only to the comment above quoted but also to subsequent comment and advice tending to create a better feeling among the employing and working classes of North Carolina.

In carrying out the plan of work of the North Carolina committee, one of the first steps was for the supervisor to inaugurate an educational campaign wherever practical among Negro workers at the various points in the State. Short itineraries were arranged and the supervisor was given permission to address groups of workers at many large plants, with specific health questions, ideals of efficiency and recreational activities, in order to preserve the morale and competency of Negro workers. Although in many instances employers had been slow to put on foot similar programs and thereby to bring about a contented group of workers, there were many leading plants in the State which had, from the beginning, recognized the need of such an institution as would make their workers contented. A superintendent of one of the large North Carolina plants had under his supervision about 800 Negro employees, who, in fact, practically made up one of the small villages of the State.   In the early formation of one of the county committees this superintendent saw a splendid opportunity presented in being able to link up his plans with the program of work of the committee.   It is of particular interest, in this connection, to point out some of the early steps which his plant had taken in an endeavor to preserve contentment among the workers.   It was estimated that the average worker at this plant in the eight-hour day was earning $100 a month.   The work was not exhausting, physically, and overtime pay was allowed to good workers. The plant in question was equipped with steel lockers, porcelain washbowls, shower baths, and other facilities necessary to the comfort and cleanliness of its workers, white and colored.   Within the village row after row of new houses had been erected.   These houses were modern and sanitary, with running water, sewerage, and electric lights. They were rented to workers at an extremely low price and many had been purchased on a ten-year plan which the company had arranged in order to increase the desire for permanent residence.   The company also paid for a nine-months school for the children of workers.   In the village itself Negroes were engaged in business enterprises which were largely patronized by workers of this plant. A modern hospital was in the course of erection and two churches had been planned.

The local Negro workers' advisory committee, under the direction of the supervisor, assisted this plant in a further educational campaign to promote efficiency and thrift among the Negro workers. Intelligent and self-respecting workers were solicited and the eventual outcome of assistance given by the local committee resulted in the company's retaining a permanent social worker who has charge of a program in behalf of the welfare of these workers.

As the work of the supervisor of Negro economics and the Negro workers' advisory committee increased in scope and understanding, various firms called upon the supervisor and his assistant for advice in the formation of plans for the higher economic status of their workers. One exceptionally large plant invited the supervisor and the director of Negro economics to outline a complete program of welfare for its Negro employees.   Such a plan was made up and submitted, and it received the commendation and adoption of the officials of the firm.

In his itineraries the assistant supervisor of Negro economics carried the program of the department into the following cities: Durham, Badin, Oxford, Henderson, Bricks, Tarboro, Dover, New Bern, Burlington, Lexington, Spencer, Charlotte, Statesville, Hickory, Morganton, Marion, Asheville, Winston-Salem, Salisbury, Raleigh, and High Point.   At various other points the supervisor and his assistant visited Negro schools, making addresses and increasing the desire of workers for greater efficiency and of employers for greater consideration of their workers.

So pleased were the governor and other State officials with the work of the Division of Negro Economics that the governor called, for June 14, 1919, the annual meeting of the Negro workers' advisory committee, at which time the State supervisor submitted his recommendations concerning the work. Inasmuch as that report received the universal commendation of persons throughout the State, it is given in full:

[U. S. Department of Labor, Office of Supervisor of Negro Economics for North Carolina, Durham, N. C.]

HOW TO KEEP NEGRO LABOR.

New methods.—How to keep the Negro workers and make them satisfied with their lot is the problem now presented to the South. It ought not be difficult of solution. It is not natural for the Negroes to leave their old homes in this wholesale fashion, and they really do not want to go. Some planters and industrial establishments are already demonstrating by means of better pay and greater care for their employees what such considerations will do in keeping the Negroes loyally at work in the South; and the more efficient Negro schools have for years been pointing the way.

Constructive possibilities.—The improvement of race relations is a matter of time, and rests largely on the satisfactory solution of the economic problems of farm life. Several noteworthy tendencies were, however, noticeably strengthened by the loss of Negro labor. The first of these was the tendency of the leaders of the two races to draw closer together. Several State-wide and county meetings were held to discuss the migration and the grievances of the Negro. Until more interest is taken in these meetings by the white leaders, and until they are followed by constructive programs for better law enforcement and education they can not measurably influence the tendency of the Negro to move.

Holding Negro labor on the farm.—There is a general agreement that friendly personal interest, absolutely fair dealing in all business transactions, clear understanding of the terms of the contract at the outset, itemized statements of indebtedness, good housing, and encouragement of the Negroes to raise their foodstuffs as far as possible, taken together, will attract and hold labor on farms.

Majority of Negroes are workers.—Since the great majority of Negroes are in the working class, their permanent interests are as laborers, and these interests are in the maintenance of living wages and of good working conditions.

The Negro's value to North Carolina.—There is no question as to the value of the Negro to the South; but circumstances are bringing other sections to an appreciation of his value also and the Negro, too, is coming to uderstand something of his worth to the community. If North Carolina would keep the Negro and have him satisfied she must give more constructive thought than has been her custom to the Negro and his welfare.

The outline of facts stated above should help us to approach our local problems with greater understanding, greater sympathy, and a great willingness to cooperate in their satisfactory adjustment. With this understanding and sympathy we are better able to appreciate the statesmanlike policy of the Department of Labor in creating and maintaining the work of Negro economics.

On May 1, 1918, the Secretary of Labor, Hon. William B. Wilson, realizing that the Negro constitutes about one-seventh of the total working population of the country, appointed a Negro, Dr. George E. Haynes, as advisory to the Secretary with the title Director of Negro Economics. This was done in order that the Negro might have a representative in council whenever matters affecting his welfare were being considered; and that more extensive plans might be developed for improving his efficiency and production in agriculture and industry.

There were appointed in four Southern States and five Northern States supervisors of Negro economics who have established cooperative committees of representative white and colored citizens to work out together the local labor problems. These Negro workers' advisory committees, as they are called, have a program of work which is carried on by the colored members, the whites serving as cooperating members. So successful has the work of the committees proved that the Division of Negro Economics have been continued for the important work of reconstruction. This work is not separate from the other work of the department, but is carried on as an integral part. The supervisors are under the authority of the Federal directors of the United States Employment Service.

North Carolina led the way.—On June 19, 1918, Gov. T. W. Bickett, called a conference in his office which was attended by 17 of the most substantial Negro citizens from all parts of the State and 5 white citizens. Out of this meeting came the plan of Negro workers' advisory committees, which is now operating in nine States. A State Negro workers' committee of leading Negro men and women of North Carolina was appointed and plans were formed for the creation of county and city committees. There were on April 1 of the present year 25 of these committees actively at work in our State.

The supervisor's report.—The supervisor of Negro Economics for North Carolina and the assistant supervisor have visited 23 counties since their organization, holding conferences with leading white and colored citizens which have been most helpful. On the basis of this personal investigation throughout the State, the supervisor wishes to present under separate headings, a summary of conditions as found:

White employers and liberal white citizens.—There is the greatest cordiality and willingness to cooperate upon the part of these persons. In many instances they rivaled the colored citizens in spirit and enthusiasm. They spoke freely as well as the Negroes, and are asking on every hand to be called upon for cooperation. Some of them came from the rural districts and from near-by towns to attend the conferences.

Many employers are already offering special inducements to their Negro workers. For example, a cotton oil company is giving free life insurance for $500 to all who remain in its employ for six months; many older employees have been given free insurance for $1,000. Knitting mill companies are carefully selecting colored girls for their plants and are giving employment at good wages throughout the year. Lumber companies are giving bonuses to men who go to the lumber camps.

The labor situation in North Carolina.—Broadly speaking there is a scarcity of Negro labor in the State. All the industries are feeling this at present. But a greater suffering will be felt in the fall when it is time for crop gathering. The farmers are suffering most. Cotton is standing in the fields in all parts of the State from last year.

It is highly desirable that leaders of white workmen cooperate with our committees.

SPECIAL PROBLEMS INVOLVING NEGRO LABOR.

1. Tobacco, guano, and cotton-oil industries. Tobacco work is seasonal; the wages are high and no great intelligence is required for much of the work. When the great warehouses open, crowds of workers leave year-round industries, often demoralizing the latter. The work of the industries here mentioned is dirty and does not invite workers of any particular skill. It is hard to promote cleanliness, efficiency, and thrift among workers whose lives are haphazard, who come and go through the streets in their working clothes and who are not generally considered as advanced workers.

2. Many of the seasonal plants run 12-hour shifts, often doubling the work day of the most faithful employees. This leads to the workers "laying off" on Saturdays and Mondays. In one 12-hour plant visited the colored workers had "struck" for Saturdays off.

3. Lumber camps: In some instances the quarters provided for logging and mill camps have not attracted respectable workers and their families. "Floaters" and crap-shooters were mainly the classes who were willing to go to such camps. Their work has, of course, not been satisfactory. On the other hand, one concern visited had made its location a real community and stimulated local pride in it. The manager of this concern spoke of his success in getting and holding labor of a splendid class in his little town.

4. Hosiery mills: The plants visited are clean and sanitary, well-lighted, and safe. They pay good wages and run all the year. The owners are trying to select their workers carefully and to encourage the development of character. But very few of them have been highly successful in getting an adequate force; and most of the girls leave as soon as the tobacco work opens. Some of these plants have never been able to increase their output; and one of them is still compelled to close on Saturdays because of a general shortage of girls.

HOW OUR NEGRO WORKERS' ADVISORY COMMITTEES CAN MEET THESE PROBLEMS.

In line with our official program of work our committees should—

(1) Promote the efficiency of colored workers in order to overcome the loss from shortage of labor.

(2) Encourage the use of farm machinery to increase farm production and to create a surplus of farm labor for use in the harvest time.

(3) Prevail upon white leaders as well as white employers to cooperate with our committees.

(4) Encourage white employers in the tobacco, guano, and cotton oil industries to make the work as clean and as pleasing as possible. The installation of clothes lockers and washrooms will impress the workers with the advantage of coming and going from work in clean clothes.

(5) Advise with employers whose plants are running long hours as to whether shorter hours will not mean greater efficiency and greater regularity. Many workers are now averaging only four days a week; the proportion of "laying off" on Saturdays and Mondays is distressingly large.

(6) Pay close attention to seasonal plants, following especially shortage and surplus, and endeavoring to assist in transfer of workers to new jobs as these plants close. The United States Employment Service should be aided in recruiting Negro workers so as not to draw away workers from "year-round" industries. Reports as to shortage and surplus should be made regularly by the committeemen to the office of the supervisor so that colored workers may secure jobs without going great distances.

(7) Suggest to employers of lumber concerns the development of community life in their camps, with better housing and family settlements.

(8) Call to the attention of steady and capable young women in the community who are not employed the excellent sanitary condition of the knitting mills and opportunity for steady employment in them.

It is urgently hoped that all public spirited citizens of both races who have at heart the agricultural and industrial expansion of our State, and who realize that such expansion and development can only come through the improvement of Negro labor will sustain this far-sighted effort of the Department of Labor and will give active support to the program of work of the Division of Negro Economics, and to the undersigned,

A. M. MOORE, M. D.,
Special Agent and Supervisor
of Negro Economics for North Carolina,
Durham, N. C.

JUNE, 1919.

It is deemed to be in place to quote commendations from Hon. T. W. Bickett, governor of North Carolina, regarding the Negro economics work in his State:

There is the greatest cordiality and willingness on the part of the white employers and liberal white citizens to cooperate with the Negroes. In many instances they rival the colored citizens in spirit and enthusiasm. They speak freely and are asking on every hand to be called into cooperation. * * *

This report sets out that in many industries and on the farms intelligent efforts are being made to improve living conditions of the Negro and to afford him every incentive to put forth his very best efforts. In one plant the committee devised a plan to publish an honor roll containing the names of all Negroes who worked steadily six days in the week. Under this system the loafing list was decreased 57 per cent and there was a corresponding increase in the number of steady workers. * * *

If every man, black and white, in the United States, could read and digest this report, it would go a great way toward solving all our questions. I shall keep and use this report as a basis for my future work. * * *

The Chief Justice of the State, the Federal Director of the United States employment Service and a number of employers all expressed themselves as profoundly impressed with the scope and character of the work done by the committee.

The North Carolina Farmers' Conference on Labor Problems, held at Bricks, N. C., April 21, 1919, brought to the attention of the department its report and recommendations made to the State Negro workers' advisory committee concerning farm labor questions as they affected Negroes in the State. This report and its recommendations are deemed to be of sufficient importance to justify its inclusion in this report, and attention is therefore called to the specific conditions and recommendations of the farmers' conference.

1. Greater use of farm machinery:
   (a) This committee should encourage greater use of farm machinery as a means of creating a surplus of farm labor.
      1. The State and Federal governments should be urged to aid the farmers in securing farm tractors, ditchers, tobacco setters, potato planters, and other needed implements.
      2. The owners of adjoining farms should be encouraged to purchase machinery jointly.
2. Cooperative undertakings:
   (a) Progressive farmers are running cooperative cotton gins, sawmills, 'and warehouses and are purchasing guano and fertilizer together. Such efforts are not only meritorious as business enterprises; they often help the farmer to market his products quickly, obtain a money surplus, and improve his farm.
   (b) Cooperative harvesting should be encouraged in order to save the crops. This practice already exists in some communities.
3. Improvement o farm life:
   (a) Every possible encouragement should be given to the improvement of farm life.
      1. This committee shall cooperate with organizations forwarding "after-the-war" programs to render rural life more pleasant and profitable.
      2. Plantation owners and farmers who employ Negro enants hould be urged to provide them with good homes.
      3. Full information concerning Government Farm Loans should be secured and given to the farmers.
      4. Athletics and outdoor sports and all forms of regulated amusements should be encouraged, as well as indoor entertainments at schools and churches for winter evenings.
4. Student farm labor:
   (a) It should be the aim of this committee to divert such student labor from the cities, for the summer vacations, as can be more profitably employed on the farms.
      1. Many students are now realizing from $300 to $500 on two (2) acres of tobacco, having sufficient time left to do general farm work also.
      2. Children of farm owners or tenants farming on their own account should be encouraged to remain at home, and parents and employers who receive the services of students should make such settlements with them as will adequately provide for the next year's schooling.
5. Distribution of labor:
   (a) Efforts should be made to recruit workers for the farms when seasonal industries close in the cities.
   (b) Cooperate with the nearest United States Employment Service office.
6. Education:
   (a) White farmer and employer:
      1. White farmers and employers of Negro farm labor should be urged to cooperate with Negro farmers in promoting the common interests of the rural communities.
   (b) Negro farmer and farm laborer:
      1. Negro farmers and farm laborers should be urged to cooperate with white farmers and employers in promoting the common interests of the rural communities.
      2. Lectures in colored churches and lodges on modern farm methods, use of farm machinery, improvement of farm life, race pride, industry and thrift, etc.
      3. Farmers' conferences.
      4. "Buy-a-farm" movement.
7. Farm demonstrators:
   (a) City and county officials should be urged to provide funds for the appointment of Negro farm demonstrators.
   (b) The breeding of registered live stock should be extended under the direction of the county farm demonstrators.
   (c) Surveys should be made as to shortage and surplus of labor before planting and harvesting crops so that acreage might be reduced or extended and crops saved.

CHAPTER XVI.

REPORT OF WORK IN OHIO.

The number of Negro migrants who settled in the principal industrial centers of Ohio were large. Estimates secured upon visits to those centers by investigators of the Department of Labor in 1917 give some definite notion of these numbers. The following figures, of course, are largely general estimates and probably should be double, and, in some cases, increased to a large extent as of September 1, 1919.

Cleveland	10,000
Cincinnati	6,000
Columbus	3,000
Dayton	3,000
Toledo	3,000
Canton	3,000
Akron	3,000
Middletown	1,000
Camp Sherman, Chillicothe	2,000
Portsmouth	300
Baltimore & Ohio camps	400
Pennsylvania Railroad camps	800
Contractors	1,000
Traction companies	1,000
Total	[1]37,500

It will be noticed that Alliance, Bellaire, Hamilton, Ironton, Lima, Springfield, Steubenville, Youngstown, and Zanesville were not included in this survey. These points, as well as other cities, contained a large number of iron, steel, coal, coke, and other industries which called for the kind of labor which Negroes were readily able to supply. As the figures indicate, large numbers of Negroes migrated into Ohio and were distributed over it generally. Therefore, this State received early consideration in the program of the Department of Labor.

Organization—Supervisor of Negro economics.—The departmental State supervisor of Negro economics, Charles E. Hall, was appointed with the view of general efficiency to the department and to the State of Ohio. For more than 18 years Mr. Hall had been an employee of the Bureau of the Census in the United States Department of Commerce, and had had considerable experience in field work. He had supervised the gathering and preparation of statistical material relating to the manufacturing interests and to the Negro population in the United States. He had received special commendation from the Department of Commerce for this work. During 1916, the early period of Negro migration to the North, Mr. Hall had been detailed to the Department of Labor for field investigations. His valuable work in a report of more than ordinary worth, served as a basis for first steps by the Department of Labor.

---

[1] Negro Migration in 1916–1917, Appendix to report of Francis E. Tyson. Government Printing Office, Washington.

Being a native of the Middle West, Mr. Hall enjoyed a wide contact with public officials and representative citizen, through whom it was believed the fullest cooperation could be obtained. He took the field in Ohio on June 17, 1918, just preceding the State conference. The later success of his work gave substantial indorsement to the judgment of the department in assigning him to Ohio.

Conference on Negro labor.—Following the assignment of Supervisor Hall to the State, under the auspices of the United States Employment Service, plans for the Ohio conference on Negro labor were started with the hearty cooperation of both State and Federal officials, the State Council of National Defense and a number of private citizens and agencies. Special mention should be made of the personal interest and attention of Gov. James M. Cox and Mr. Fred D. Croxton, chairman of the State Council of National Defense.

The conference was called by the Department of Labor to get action upon those things that needed to be done in Ohio to promote the welfare of wage erners, and to stimulate the production for winning the war. Dr. F. L. Hagerty, professor of sociology, Ohio State University, presided. After considerable discussion and a number of addresses the body of the work of the conference was done, through committees, reports from which were adopted for the further guidance of the department's work in the State.

Some of the committees' recommendations were as follows;

1. Investigation into the difficulties arising from discrimination against Negroes by local labor unions.

2. Efforts to stabilize labor by giving new opportunities for promotion, by standardizing wages, by reclassifying work, by the employment of colored foremen, and by educational work among the working classes with the view of making them satisfied with their occupations.

3. An endeavor to employ the Negro worker in full accordance with his fitness.

4. The opening of new places of employment in keeping with the fitness of Negro wage-earners.

5. The conducting of welfare work in plants and factories.

6. The setting up of facilities for community recreation.

7. Increased attention to rooms, lockers, ventilation, and adequate space for employees.

8. Special attention to health problems.

The committee on industrial conditions reported to the conference that there was sufficient work to be secured in the State for Negro laborers in industry doing Government and other work and that the Negro laborers were generally reliable. It also reported that in some industries there was discrimination as to the kinds of work and conditions under which the work was done with reference to Negro laborers. The committee stated that the demand for labor was more than the supply and in order that the Government might get the greatest return out of the amount of the actual and potential energy of the Negro workmen it was recommended that where skilled Negro laborers were doing unskilled work because of their inability to secure work at the skilled trades on account of color that the Government adopt rules for governmental contracts and make a special effort to see that every such man be given the opportunity to do that for which he was best fitted. The final recommendation of this committee closed with the averment that "race or color should be no bar to advancement."

The committee on organization adopted with modifications to meet local conditions for use in Ohio the form of constitution for the Negro workers' advisory committee which the department had developed.

The committee on Negro women in industry submitted a report on this subject of such special importance for future procedure that it is reproduced here in full:

1. We, as a committee, recommend that a Negro woman be placed on the State committee of women in industry, recently named by the Ohio Branch, Council of National Defense.

2. We, as a committee, recommend that the United States Employment Service place Negro placement secretaries in any employment office where numbers of colored women seek employment, to be determined by the State director.

3. We, as a committee, recommend that we indorse the standard which the women's committee, Ohio Branch, Council of National Defense, have drawn up through the committee on women in industry.

4. We recommend that this committee bring to the attention of the national committee on housing any housing conditions as they affect Negro women.

5. We recommend that a pamphlet be drawn up stating the necessity of loyalty to duty and efficiency on the part of the worker, and the financial loss entailed through the neglect of such, upon the part of the employer and community, be given each worker through the employment office.

6. We, as a committee, recommend that a woman be placed on the committee of hygiene and sanitation, if the committee appointed this morning is a standing committee.

7. We recommend that no worker shall be permitted to leave her present employment without giving a week or more notice before being accepted by another employer.

8. We recommend and urge that a Negro welfare worker be placed in industries over Negro women as a solution to the employers' problem of adjustment.

9. We recommend the encouragement of an adequate system of training within plants which recognizes the difference between showing and teaching for all new employees.

Respectfully submitted.

Miss JENNIE D. PORTER,
Chairman, Cincinnati, Ohio.
Miss ELSIE MOUNTAIN,
Secretary, Columbus, Ohio.

Hon. James M. Cox, governor of Ohio, was present at the conference and made the closing address, which included the following remarks:

I have no disposition to interfere with your deliberations, but upon the statement of Dr. Haynes, with whom I have had a brief but delightful conference with reference to the earnestness of this meeting and the fact that it seems to be the most serious, if not the most successful, meeting that has been held in any of the States, I felt that we would be derelict in our responsibility to the duties that come and go each day, as governor of this State, if I did not come here and express my appreciation of your coming.

First, we need your people and need them badly in the war. We, likewise, need your people and need them badly in the industrial life of this country.

Last winter I had the privilege of visiting Tuskegee Institute. I had a long visit with that splendid type of your race, Dr. Moton. The opportunity was mine of making a survey of what was being done at this institute. I took pains to make considerable inquiry with reference to national and industrial conditions in the State of Alabama, and I am prepared to say, in the candor of my own judgment, at least, that you, as representatives of the race, are just now coming into your own. Even in the Southern States, when the great flow started northward, the southern people found they could not get along without the colored people.

The war gives you a great opportunity. I can say with pride, now, and reiterate it all through the corridor of time, that not a single member of your race is following the standard of the Kaiser. I have had the opportunity of reviewing colored troops, and I hope you will not feel that I am speaking flippantly when I recall the circumstances of reviewing the troops at Camp Sherman. Capt. Talbott, with Gen. Glenn's staff, came over to the reviewing stand and said: "I have just left the colored regiment, and they are so full of pep that if they do not dance the cakewalk when they come by, I will be surprised.'' They presented the best line of the day—it was generally conceded to be the best line of the day by the general, the persons in the reviewing stand, and the thousands of white people who were assembled there. I hope that when the war is over we can then join together members of our race and yours in helping to work out in Ohio what they have in Alabama.

The colored man is here, and here to stay, and since that is true we not only want to improve the educational opportunities that come to him but we also want to give attention to vocational training. * * * I want you to carry home to those you represent the assurance that whatever help this State can render, either to the people in your State or to the soldiers at the front, needs but an evidence of your desire.

The Department of Labor takes this special opportunity to thank every agency and every individual who helped to make successful the Ohio conference August 5, 1919.

Negroes workers' advisory committees.—Immediately after the conference, Supervisor Hall, with the assistance of public-spirited citizens of Ohio, recommended to the department a number of the strongest persons for appointment to service on the State Negro workers' advisory committee, and to local, county, and city committees of 25 important centers of the State where Negro workers in considerable numbers resided. The complete personnel of the State committee follows:

Edward Berry, Athens; Leroy W. Bobbins and Chas. C. Cowgill, Middletown; Chas. L. Johnson and Chas. P. Dunn, Springfield; Robert K. Hodges, D. R. Williams, Alexander H. Martin, and (Miss) Hazel Mountain, Cleveland; Chas. W. Bryant, Harry B. Alexander, J. H. Hendrick, and (Mrs.) E. W. Moore, Columbus; J. E. Ormes, Wilberforce; R. E. Holmes, Xenia; F. D. Patterson, Greenfield; Joseph L. Jones, H. S. Dunbar, Fred. A. Geier, and (Miss) Anna Laws, Cincinnati; B. M. Ward, B. H. Fisher, and (Mrs.) Minnie Scott, Toledo; Rev. W. O. Harper, and T. E. Milliken, Youngstown; H. T. Elliott, Dayton; Rev. A. M. Thomas, Zanesville; (Mrs.) Stephen Bates, Chillicothe; James French, Sandusky; T. E. Greene, Akron.

Persons serving on these committees did so at the special request of the Secretary of Labor, and, in but one or two instances, where the appointees were confronted with extreme pressure of business, were the invitations declined. Throughout the work the patriotism and spirit of service of the citizenship of Ohio made possible the successful carrying out of virtually every plan which the department launched, and the Ohio committee, like similar committees in 10 other States, assisted in the handling of industrial problems with a maximum degree of satisfaction.

Surveys of labor conditions.—The general industrial conditions in Ohio were investigated either by the supervisor directly or by the committee members, who reported to the supervisor on a form of blank, of which the following is a copy:

NEGRO WAGE EARNERS IN OHIO.

Information for supervisor of Negro economics.

To members of county and city committees of Negro workers' advisory committee.
    Please fill out blank and return.
    1. Are there many out of work in your city or county? ———.
    2. Have many been released during the past 30 days? ———.
    3. If so, were they absorbed by other occupations? ———.
    4. Have any new avenues of employment been opened? ———.
    5. If so, state the kind of work. ———.

Remarks.

(Under "Remarks" please furnish the supervisor with any other information which you think should be brought to his attention.)

Information furnished by ....

Address: ....

Date: ....

The first general survey developed the following facts:

The Negro workers had not been greatly disturbed because of the many industrial readjustments and temporary suspensions of the manufacturing enterprises not essential to winning the war, during the war and preceding the signing of the armistice.

The counties of Hamilton, Lucas, and Montgomery, whose principal cities are Cincinnati, Toledo, and Dayton, respectively, were largely engaged on war contracts. In Toledo the opportunities for employment were steadily improving. Local industries in Cleveland, Columbus, Youngstown, Akron, Canton, Lima, Delaware, Greenville, Steubenville, Zanesville, Chillicothe, Sandusky, Portsmouth, Marietta, and other centers were employing large numbers of Negro workers. In Butler County, the American Rolling Mills were giving employment to hundreds of workers. In Lima, the Swift Packing Co. was giving employment to Negro men and women, who were making good. In Youngstown, Mahoning County, an increasing number of elevator girls and male truck drivers were given employment.

In Dayton a large firm was making calls for considerable numbers of Negro laborers. This company was able to guarantee prospective workers housing facilities of the better type. Columbus reported a garment manufacturer who was unable to get a sufficient number of Negro women who could operate power machines. Youngstown reported insufficient wages ($9 and $10 a week) for girls. Dayton reported an industry using from 15 to 30 colored women, sorting rags on a piecework basis, at $15 per week.

Job selling.—Among the special conditions found in Ohio was one which related to job selling in industrial establishments; and there is incorporated herein a full report of the Ohio supervisor respecting this condition, evidences of which were very apparent. This report was approved by the Director of Negro Economics and sent to advisory committeemen in all parts of the State.

JOB SELLING IN INDUSTRIAL ESTABLISHMENTS TO NEGROES.

To prevent job selling by foremen, assistant foremen, "straw bosses" and "go-betweens" a very comprehensive bill was enacted by the last General Assembly upon the recommendation of the Industrial Commission of Ohio, the penalty being as follows:

"SECTION 2. Whoever violates any provision of this act shall be fined for the first offense not less than one hundred dollars nor more than five hundred dollars and the costs of prosecution; and for the second or any subsequent offense not less than two hundred dollars nor more than one thousand dollars and the costs of prosecution."

"SECTION 6. The Industrial Commission of Ohio shall have full power, jurisdiction, and authority to administer the provisions of this act."

Before the migration of Negroes from the South had reached a considerable volume, the foreign-born wage earners were the ones who were the victims of this pernicious system and the Department of Investigation and Statistics secured definite information that the collection of fees for jobs, or assessments of various kinds by foremen was a well-established custom in many of the industrial establishments through the State. It was found at the time the investigation was made that the price paid to foremen was generally $15, $20, or $25 for a job paying approximately 25 cents per hour, and that the custom appeared to have become so well established that no demand for payment needed to be made as the applicant understood that he must make a payment of money before he got the work.

Definite information was secured by the department to the effect that the shrewd foreman seldom received the money directly from the applicant, but usually had a number of men who acted as "go-betweens" and who were generally "straw bosses" or workmen.

This system of petty graft became so pronounced and the demands of the grafters became so insistent that the investigators experienced no great difficulty in securing the evidence upon which a number of indictments were made under the old law relating to private employment agencies which was not broad enough in scope, however, to fit the entire situation.

The new law includes the acceptance of fees, gifts or gratuities, or promises to pay a fee or to make a gift under the agreement or with the understanding that the grafter will undertake to secure or assist in securing work for the applicant, or with the understanding that he will advance or undertake to secure or assist in securing an advance in pay or prevent or undertake to prevent or assist in preventing the discharge or reduction in pay or position of the worker in the employ of the company. The law which was enacted by the eighty-second general assembly covers all of these points and carries with it the penalty indicated above.

There are indication that there has been a revival of the practice of job selling, but that instead of working on the foreigners, the grafters have turned their attention to the helpless, ignorant, and destitute Negroes who are coming from the South to seek opportunities to better their condition, and it is not unlikely that the system of job selling in industrial establishments in Ohio will again be investigated as the practice is not only unlawful and highly dishonorable but has a tendency to destroy the morale of the workers and thereby seriously affect production. All such cases should be reported.

CHARLES E. HALL,
Supervisor of Negro Economics.

Approved.

(Signed)   GEORGE E. HAYNES,
Director of Negro Economics.

Living conditions of Negro workers.—It was the experience of the department that unfavorable living conditions, more than anything else, made difficult the advancement of the Negro worker in efficiency and increased contentment. At times the housing conditions were due to lack of employment; at times the conditions were due to lack of pride on the part of the worker; and at times the boarding-house keeper of the low type set up conditions which necessity forced the working men to accept.

As to the latter class, in one instance Supervisor Hall reported as follows:

OCTOBER 11, 1918.

Dr. GEORGE E. HAYNES,
Director of Negro Economics, Department of Labor, Washington, D. C.

DEAR SIR: On the evening of October 9, 1918, I visited the boarding and lodging house conducted by ———— ————, a colored man, for the ———— Co., ————, Ohio.

This very dilapidated two-story frame building is located at ———— Street, and is known as ————. It is the most filthy boarding and lodging house that has come under my observation. A foul-smelling closet adjoins the unclean dining room. I noticed broken windows upstairs in the sleeping quarters, and in the south wing even the skylights were without glass or other protection from the elements.

There is no shower or bathroom for the 42 men who occupy this house, and it has been found necessary to borrow a washtub from the neighbors to accommodate the men who wish to take a bath. The place is heated by small stoves and natural gas heaters and the building is lighted by electricity. The kitchen was fairly clean but the range had no hot-water boiler, which greatly inconveniences the cooks and other kitchen help as well as the boarders.

A number of the dirty sunken floors need jacking up and the rooms would not be less attractive if they were painted or whitewashed. Although there are a few new bed mattresses, I found most of them alarmingly filthy with bed coverings in the same condition. Although there are plenty of rooms in the house, many of them are unfurnished. Upon inquiry I was informed that the men coming off the night shift are obliged to occupy the rooms just vacated by the men going on the day shift. In some instances four of five men sleep in a room about 10 by 12 at the same time. Some of the bed springs are worn out, necessitating the sleeper to lie in most uncomfortable positions, regardless of the fact that he has been working hard and that the efficiency of his work depends largely upon comfortable repose. There is no assembly room, music (except nickel-in-the-slot piano), pool, billiards, or books.

For these most inferior accommodations the men are charged $7.25 per week for room and board as compared with $4.55 per week charged by the ——— Co., located in the same city and within a few blocks. The ——— Co. maintains a large boarding and lodging house, known as "The ———," which is now being papered, painted, and generally overhauled.

In my opinion, the ——— is extremly insanitary and a disease breeder, a condition which could not have escaped the attention of the local officials of the company, one of whom visits the house daily for the purpose of checking up.

These conditions are doubtless the causes of the large turnover and inefficiency of the colored workers of this company.

Respectfully,

CHARLES E. HALL,
Supervisor of Negro Economics, Ohio.

This report was approved by the Director of Negro Economics for submission to the general manager of the ——— Company. Subsequent action by the company in the renovation of this place and change of these conditions followed the receipt of this report by him.

Critical housing conditions in Cleveland, together with other economic problems, gave to that city a special need which the department planned to give attention to through a local representative member of the Negro workers' advisory committee. This plan, however, was delayed and finally given up because of necessary changes in the policy of the department.

Acute housing conditions were found also at Akron, Cleveland, Dayton, Lima, Portsmouth, Toledo, and Youngstown; and, subsequently, the Department of Labor, through the United States Housing Corporation, had surveys made in several of these cities, but the sudden termination of the war, accompanied by a readjustment of the industries to a peace-time basis, threw a great many persons out of work and the housing condition was somewhat relieved through the general exodus of Negro and white wage earners to other localities within and without the State where there was a shortage of labor and where adequate housing facilities obtained. One permanent result in stimulating building and loan associations is fully described below.

The failure of congressional appropriations for the furtherance of the Negro economics work unfavorably affected the industrial progress of this class of wage earners who had watched with increasing interest the development of this new agency which was established to better their industrial welfare and to act as a clearing house for industrial opportunities. Men were no longer obliged to live in idleness, because they were able at all times to learn through the supervisor where work could be obtained, the rate of wages, the hours of labor, and the attitude of the residents of any community toward Negro labor. Negro professional men, skilled and unskilled workers, and others, freely communicated with the Director of Negro Economics and with the State supervisor for the purpose of securing a location or an opportunity in a community where conditions were favorable to their prosperity, and the failure of appropriations to provide for the continuance of this field work was keenly felt.

Discrimination in occupations on account of color was one of the conditions which, in some instances, confronted the Negro worker. The Ohio Conference on Negro Labor made recommendations on this point. Whether such discriminations were approved by private or public employers made a difference in the action which the department could take. The private employer might hire whomsoever he chose. Aside from an appeal for justice and fair play on his part, the department was unable to take any specific action in such cases. Where such discriminations, however, were alleged to exist within the ranks of employers who because of war contracts or other relations came under the jurisdiction of the Federal Government, investigations were made and definite steps taken to remove such discriminations.

Complaints.—Complaints, other than those noted above, were generally of three types:

1. Discrimination in the matter of opportunities for the Negro worker.
2. Unfair treatment of the Negro worker by employers.
3. Inefficiency of the Negro workers.

On the whole, there was a minimum amount of complaint in Ohio either by employer or employee. The stamp of efficiency was often placed upon the Negro worker, and the Negro worker often recognized the effort on the part of employers assuring to him equal pay, equal hours, recreation facilities, pleasant relations with white workers, and decent living conditions.

Results.—Under the supervision of the United States Employment Service, the State supervisor of Negro economics made direct reports of placement of Negro workers to the Federal director. He assisted the employment offices throughout the State with their problems of placing Negro workers. Reports of the United States Employment Service give him the recognition for this help. Placements were many and varied. Services were frequently rendered to firms which had not formerly employed Negro workers. Following the signing of the armistice and the resulting nonemployment situation the efforts for the returning Negro soldiers and sailors were carried along side by side with the efforts of the Federal and State machinery for the employment of all persons.

An outstanding feature of the Ohio work was the project of furthering the organization of building and loan associations among Negroes of the State as one concrete means of remedying the housing situation. In a letter dated May 8, 1919, which was given State-wide publicity, Supervisor Hall made the following points:

1. Industrial opportunities in Ohio are ever opening.
2. The housing facilities offered to Negro workers are inadequate.
3. Negro people themselves should make some of the financial arrangements for meeting the housing situation.
4. Overcrowded and insanitary housing conditions destroy the efficiency of the worker.
5. The home owner is ever a permanent working factor, contributing to the growth of the State and to its civic and commercial progress.

Thereafter Supervisor Hall compiled, from the Laws of Ohio, a skeleton outline of the statutes regulating the organizing and conducting of building and loan associations. He also formed a plan and model constitution for such associations among colored people of the several localities. This outline of laws and plans was placed in the hands of members of the Negro workers' advisory committees and of special groups in the cities and counties throughout the State having a considerable Negro population. This was supplemented by talks made by the supervisor to interested groups in various places. Wilberforce University gave special courses of lectures on building and loan matters in three centers of the State. So numerous became the requests for additional information that the supervisor found it necessary to prepare a model form of constitution and by-laws for distribution. In rapid succession building and loan associations were organized in several Ohio cities where they are greatly needed. Requests for the "Ohio plan" were also made by persons living in Colorado, District of Columbia, Georgia, Maryland, Michigan, and New York, and several associations in these States have since been organized. All are reported to be doing good business financially and are helping to alleviate the housing conditions. Companies in other places are proposed and will doubtless be launched.

In carrying out the purpose with which it was charged by Congress, the Department of Labor has steadfastly been a neutral administrator regarding union and nonunion workers, and has endeavored to promote alike the interests of all workers, white and colored, male and female, union and nonunion. With this in view, the department has sought to keep fully informed of the attitude of labor organizations toward Negroes in territories where the question is a vital one for amicable relations of the two races in industry.

Consequently, statement of the change in the attitude of organized labor in Ohio during this period is of special note. The copy of a letter of Mr. Thomas J. Donnelly, secretary-treasurer, Ohio Federation of Labor, outlining the attitude of that organization in the matter of unionizing Negro wage earners covers this important point:

Columbus, Ohio, *January 22, 1919.*

Mr. Chas. E. Hall,
   Supervisor of Negro Economics,
      Department of Labor, Columbus, Ohio.

Dear Mr. Hall: Supplementing our conversation recently upon the subject of Negro labor and the unionizing of colored men in this section of the country, I am writing you that at this time best results would be obtained, in my opinion, if efforts should be made to bring into the union those colored men who were born and educated in the North, where through contact and association with the whites they have formed the same viewpoint on industrial affairs, see the same necessity for a sustained effort, have the same "pep," and the same determination to protect their rights as wage earners and as citizens. These men can be taken in by the organizations representing both the skilled and unskilled branches of the labor unions, and I believe that no great objection would be found, especially if in communities where there are large numbers of both white and colored, distinct locals were organized; but where there are only a few whites or a few colored men following the same trade it would be advisable for them to belong to the same local. A possible objection to a mixed local in communities where there are large numbers of both races employed in the same line of work is that both elements might vote along the color line upon questions of organization and policies. This of course would have a tendency to destroy the solidarity of the organization and to discount its work. I believe that once these colored workers were fairly well organized they would be a valued aid in organizing the illiterate ones who have migrated from the South and give them a clearer view of northern ideals and the responsibilities accompanying citizenship.

While it has been my experience that colored men as a rule make good union men, I do not think that the colored agricultural illiterates from the South are adaptable to skilled industry and membership in unions of the skilled white workers.

Negroes reared in Ohio, having the advantage of the public schools in the State, should be adaptable to skilled industry and no doubt could secure membership in the unions of the skilled white workers or have separate organizations chartered by the international trades-unions. Places could possibly be found for a number of southern colored agricultural illiterates at common labor and in semiskilled trades. They would then be eligible to membership in the unions of the workers in these lines of industry.

Improved machinery has greatly lessened the demand for muscle, but at the same time has increased the demand for men who are trained to use their heads as well as their hands.

A great number of accidents in the Ohio factories and mills during the past few years has largely been due to the employment of illiterate foreigners from southern Europe, who formerly followed agricultural pursuits, and the employment of large numbers of Negroes of the same class from the South would result, no doubt, in a like number of accidents. Until they become factory broken, more punctual and dependable in attendance, more intelligent, and more accustomed to the northern method of living they will not really constitute an asset of large value to skilled industry.

Yours, very truly,

THOS. J. DONNELLY,
Secretary-Treasurer, Ohio State Federation of Labor.

In closing the work in Ohio, after the failure of appropriations, Supervisor Hall gave the following statement of concrete results of his efforts:

1. The growth and stimulation of the opinion among colored workers that the Government has recognized them industrially, that they now have a medium through which to voice their complaints, and that because of the moral effect of such recognition they will be less subject to exploitation.

2. A more helpful attitude on the part of employers and a less hostile one on the part of white wage earners brought about through contact with colored members of committees.

3. The gradual elimination of racial objection at "the gate" or point of hiring, through the cultivation of superintendents, managers, and directors of employment.

4. The announcement of the official attitude of the Ohio State Federation of Labor concerning skilled and unskilled Negro labor.

5. The increase in efficiency and decrease in labor turnover brought about through the knowledge or belief that they would be given a "square deal" industrially.

6. The awakening of Negroes, through the circulation of frequent State-wide reports, to the industrial opportunities open to them.

7. The location, through questionnaires sent to county committees, of points where a surplus or shortage of Negro labor obtained, and the adjustment of these conditions, when possible, through the Clearance Division of the United States Employment Service.

8. The placing of movable wooden racks on cold cement floors of shower baths in several industrial plants in order to encourage a more frequent use of the bath.

9. The closing of several dilapidated, filthy, disease-breeding Negro boarding and lodging houses maintained by large manufacturing companies. The personal inspection of other lodging houses, camps, etc.

10. The creation of a better understanding of the functions of the Department of Labor, and a greater appreciation of governmental agencies brought about through the efforts of the State and county Negro worker's advisory committees.

11. The development of cooperative groups through the encouragement and information given to committees in communities where the organization of a building and loan association would be both practicable and advisable.

12. The appointment of several colored "labor scouts" whose efficient work in congested industrial centers was of great value to the service and to the Negro wage earners.

The opinions and attitude of white and colored citizens of Ohio on the work of Negro economics in that State show something of its effect. A few excerpts from the communications to the department are given below:

Your circular with reference to Negro economics in Ohio under date of December 14th was received by us and read with lively interest. Any further communication or publication you may have on this subject I am sure will be appreciated. We are interested in this problem as you are, and desire to help in its solution so far as it is possible for us to do so.

I am glad to know that your work is progressing satisfactorily. I sincerely hope that we will continue to hold our own industrially, and that the Government will continue to cooperate with us and allow us representation in the Department of Labor.

_____

I shall be glad to cooperate with you to the extent of my ability in trying to bring about the conditions we both desire during readjustment.

_____

I received your circular, and most heartily welcome its coming. Words are inadequate to express my appreciation. Please let the good thing continue to come this way.

_____

The work you are in calls for a first-class race man's efforts, and I believe that you should be retained with the Government in the same capacity. I am pleased to have met you, to have learned of your work, and to have been brought in touch with it, and I believe you will be successful.

_____

I am glad you have completed your organization, and I assure you you have my full support.

_____

In returning your information blank, I would state that the United States Employment Service is filling a long-felt need among our people, and that your methods meet my approval and will receive my earnest support. Let me hear from you at any time.

_____

Congratulations on your report. Keep it up. Just simply the information is a tremendous factor in cementing the race, and that means ultimate solidarity and success.

_____

Your very concise and yet informative letter relative to labor and labor conditions among the Negroes came to hand. It is a splendid document. You are to be congrautlated upon its production, for in it you have at your finger tips the best and most information it has been my good fortune to receive relative to the Negro in this important field of endeavor in Ohio. I wish you continued success in all your efforts.

_____

I thank you for the circular letter concerning the readjustment of Negro labor. Keep me posted, and if I can serve you, call on me.

_____

We have also got good service from the United States Employment Service, and Mr. Hall, State supervisor, is doing a great work.

_____

I wish to congratulate you upon the excellent work you are doing in Ohio for the industrial advancement of our people. We all appreciate the opportunity to cooperate with you and the Department of Labor.

_____

Your letter with the inclosed statement marked "Personal, not for publication" has been received. We are grateful to you for your kindness in sending this information.

_____

I wish to advise you that as a result of your efforts here in Cincinnati to organize a building and loan association managed by colored men, we have the Industrial Savings & Loan Co., incorporated for $300,000, which commenced doing business January 31. We will be prepared to make our first loan within the next week or 10 days and our prospects are very bright for a large and growing company.

CHAPTER XVII.

REPORT OF WORK IN PENNSYLVANIA.

Pre war Conditions.—Negro labor can not be said to have enjoyed any abnormal inclusion in Pennsylvania industries. The historical and political development of Pennsylvania has not been such as to attract a large Negro population. Pennsylvania labor was probably formed, largely, by foreigners comprised of the so-called "Hunkie" laborer in the unskilled and semiskilled occupations. The skilled class was probably made up of American labor which developed in Pennsylvania along with the development of industry and which was supplemented, under the law of demand and supply, by skilled artisans and mechanics who came into Pennsylvania from other centers. Even the Negro mining class had been employed, previous to the war, in fairly large proportions in Pennsylvania mining districts of the southwestern section. In the Pittsburgh district, more than in any other section, the Negro worker, before the war, probably enjoyed a greater inclusion into all branches of labor than he did at any other point in the State.

The Pittsburgh Negro had long since become a very desirable citizen, a competent worker, and a thrifty individual. In the steel mills at Pittsburgh, "rollers" and other types of workers were employed at salaries sometimes as large as $250 per month. These persons maintained good homes and contributed to a high type of civic life in Pittsburgh. Now and then a technical worker from some of the best American universities was in a supervisory position in a steel mill.

Industrial advances during the war.—With the stress of war the great industries of Pennsylvania, through sheer necessity, became objective centers of a tremendously large mass of workers. The never-failing law of demand and supply was exercising great influence in drawing laborers. To the Negro worker, whether he came from locations within the State of Pennsylvania or other Northern States, or from the South, which was pouring into northern industries its thousands of Negro migrants, the influence of the law of demand and supply was very effective. Consequently Negro labor of every type was drawn into employment in Pennsylvania, from Philadelphia to Pittsburgh.

When the Division of Negro Economics was established, the plans of the Secretary of Labor called for the development of this work of the Negro, choosing first the points of the greatest needs in different sections of the country. For this reason the work of the division was somewhat delayed in its beginning in Pennsylvania.

The machinery of the United States Employment Service had been well established in Pennsylvania and as soon as plans for the Negro work were perfected and a worker available, it was decided to establish a cooperating office, first, at Erie, Pa. A competent Negro official, Harry E. Arnold, of the United States Employment Service, was accordingly detailed to that city.

At that time Erie presented some very critical problems affecting the relations of white and Negro workers. At the outset of the war there was said to be about 300 Negroes residing in Erie. But on November 18, 1918, this population had increased to 2,000 persons, the majority of them newcomers, practically all of whom had come from the South. Housing conditions most seriously affected the Negroes in Erie. When the Negro economics activities first looked in upon the situation, 200 Negro laborers were living in crowded bunk houses and hastily erected camps. The larger portion of Negro female workers were employed in domestic and personal service. Considerable complaint on the part of employees was directed against "irregularity of service." Because of this and the housing conditions, there was a large turnover of labor in Erie, male and female.

Organization of committees.—The Negro special agent, Harry E. Arnold, following the above-described plan of the Secretary of Labor, through the Director of Negro Economics, established a strong committee of colored and cooperating white members in Erie. The purposes and functions of such a committee have been previously explained. A labor survey of Erie followed and thereafter, as soon as the local situation had been well got in hand, similar plans were outlined for Meadville, Sharon, Pittsburgh, Washington, Connellsville, Harrisburg, New Castle, Beaver Falls, Sewickley, Wilkinsburg, Braddock, Homestead, Monongahela, Uniontown, Johnstown, Steelton, Carlisle, Chambersburg, York, Gettysburg, Williamsport, Lancaster, Coatesville, Scranton, and other industrial centers.

The signing of the armistice, of course, made unnecessary a greater development of plans for Negro labor in Pennsylvania, but during December, 1918, and January, February, and March, 1919, the Negro special agent had carried forward such plans in order to meet the readjustments which would naturally be found in reconstruction times. The beginning of April, 1919, found a surplus of 100 unemployed Negroes in Erie. The special agent within a few weeks had assisted in reducing this surplus to 48. In this effort it was necessary for him to seek opportunities and assistance from a number of plants in the placement of Negro workers. Thirty-one representative plants, principally in the iron and steel industries, gave ready attention to the employment of Negro labor, and the following facts are significant in connection with its greater inclusion in Pennsylvania industries: Four hundred colored men, of which 50 per cent were skilled workers, were employed in one of the railroad shops. Six of these employees were rated as "first-class mechanics" and were ranked among the most efficient in the shops. The officials of a metal company and of a boiler company, both of which employed foundry men and skilled workers, stated that their "Negro employees are as efficient as the whites."

When it became necessary for these plants to reduce their forces on account of the cancellation of contracts, preference was given, in the matter of continuation, to the permanent residents of the localities wherein these industries had their plants. The result was that the permanent employees are old residents of that city. This, of course, assists in stimulating the continuance of home ownership and solidarity of civic life. The special agent reported 200 Negroes in the employ of the Carnegie Steel Co. on May 7, 1918. Prior to the signing of the armistice the number was probably from 600 to 800.

In this instance, inadequate housing again retarded the inclusion of skilled workers. Bunk houses and other unsatisfactory conditions which the better type of laborer would be discontented with estopped supply of the skilled Negro worker. The American Steel & Wire Co. reported a regular force of 75 Negro workers, practically all of whom were skilled employees. The Savage Arms Corporation reported 60 colored workers on Government contracts. Two machinists were included in this number.

The above facts show to a small degree some of the practical work accomplished by this division within a very short period of time. The adjustments which followed the appointment of a departmental representative in Pennsylvania indicate the need of the continuation of such a special service in Pennsylvania districts, in which the Negro worker is striving for a permanent place in the industrial life. It may well be said that the great opportunities in this great State will at least, in some small degree, be more readily available to the competent Negro worker of the future.

Cooperation.—The Division of Negro Economics is particularly grateful to the private individuals and organizations in Pennsylvania, as well as public officials, Federal, State, and city, who cooperated wholeheartedly in the work. Of particular mention are the Pittsburgh Urban League, the Interstate Industrial Arts Association, and the Armstrong Association of Philadelphia. These organizations, with their wealth of material knowledge regarding Negro life, were quick to come to the assistance of the department in this special effort. The Negro Workers' Advisory Committee of Philadelphia, comprised of strong white and colored citizens of that city, was. made possible through the activities and help of the two last-named organizations. This committee, seated at Philadelphia, a point in which Negro life is very important, would have done inestimable work of value for the department had the future allowed a continuance of the complete field work of the Negro Economics Service.

As this report goes to the press, a statement has come from Erie, Pa., to the effect that the Negro workers' advisory committee of that city is still holding regular meetings, in an advisory capacity, with regard to the present labor problems of that vicinity. This is of special significance in view of the fact that nearly a year has elasped since the permanent work conducted by the department at Erie, ceased to function. The statement referred to emphasizes a cordial racial relationship at Erie and bespeaks a high respect on the part of employers and employees, white and colored, for the results accomplished by the committee.

CHAPTER XVIII.

REPORT OF WORK IN VIRGINIA.

The work of organization in this State was very easily launched after conference with the executive committee of the Negro Organization Society, which already had branch organizations in many localities of the State, both rural and city. The executive secretary of the State National Council of Defense very readily approved of our plans and directed the chairmen of the county councils throughout the State to appoint three white representatives for service as cooperating members for our local Negro workers' advisory committees. We soon had, therefore, committees established in about 60 counties and 5 cities of the State and an office established at Richmond with Mr. T. C. Erwin, formerly executive secretary of the Negro Organization Society, in charge.

A series of local conferences between white employers and Negro workers for making out plans and adjustment of misunderstandings were held in Richmond, Alexandria, Roanoke, Norfolk, Petersburg, and Portsmouth. A special note may be given of the cooperative action of the State Council of National Defense in dealing successfully with a very critical situation of friction between white and colored carpenters at Camp Lee.

One of the outstanding results of these conferences was the handling of an apparent labor shortage at Norfolk. The following is a brief statement of facts: The chamber of commerce discovered that many activities of the city on which Governmental projects depended was suffering from lack of labor. At the same time there seemed to be large numbers of able-bodied men in the city. The labor shortage committee was appointed and an announcement made that there would be a campaign of officers of the law to compel men to go to work or to go to jail. As this affected Negro workers very largely, Mr. P. B. Young, chairman of the Negro workers' advisory committee took up the question with the labor shortage committee, pointing out to them that such a plan would not serve to get workers but to drive them from the city. A substitute plan was offered by the advisory committee to carry on an educational campaign, laying before the workers at mass meetings the labor shortage confronting the community and its meaning to the city and to the Government, with an appeal for volunteers. This plan was agreed to, and a series of street addresses were made at night on the most popular street corners in the districts frequented by Negroes. After a ten days' campaign of this kind employment offices were overrun with volunteer workers and there were more men than were needed on the jobs.

The office of the supervisor received regular reports from over the State of the Negro labor situation and gave special assistance as a result in meeting the farm labor shortage wherever possible. Special educational campaigns were carried on throughout the State by means of bulletins giving information to the local committees on war labor needs and furnishing material on employment, health, housing, and recreation that might be passed to the congregations within the territory of each committee.

The supervisor of Negro economics was also associated with the director of the Boys' Working Reserve for the State of Virginia, and directed the beginning of that work among colored boys of the State to assist in supplying the farm labor shortage during the farming season of 1918 and the spring season of 1919.

When the Housing Bureau proposed the establishment of a model community at Truxtun, the supervisor of Negro economics very early was in touch with some of the strong colored citizens of Portsmouth, near by. A Negro workers' advisory committee, with Mr. W. H. Jennings as chairman, was formed. Through them there was developed contact with the officers of the navy yards, and the Housing Corporation was assisted in getting suitable residents for the houses of the project when opened.

A few weeks after the first blocks of houses were occupied there appeared need for continued assistance in getting these residents adjusted to the new community and in securing cooperation among the families. The supervisor of Negro economics for Virginia therefore gave considerable attention to this in cooperation with the local advisory committee of Portsmouth for help in stimulating the pride of the new residents in their community and in efforts to make Truxtun a model in every respect by keeping the buildings in the model condition they were when first occupied, and the lawns and surrounding grounds in first-class condition.

After a few weeks it became evident that it was desirable to have a Negro operating representative put in charge of the project. The United States Housing Corporation appointed Mr. Fred D. McCracken, who had been with the Housing Bureau for more than a year, first as assistant to the chief of the United States Homes Registration and Placement Service, in Washington, and later as a traveling representative of the United States Housing Corporation. Mr. McCracken took charge as operating representative of Truxtun in July, 1919.

This Truxtun project consists of 254 family houses with modern improvements, including electricity, hot and cold water, with garden and lawn space for each house, all being either detached or semi-detached residences. There are four stores and a modern brick school with 10 rooms all on one floor.

Not only did the operating representative get the support of the Negro Workers' Advisory Committee of Portsmouth, but he soon formed an association of the householders of the community, dividing the town into districts, with a captain over each district. These captains formed a sort of town council for advice and help to the manager in directing the affairs of the town.

The project, under his management, has continued with marked success, including the conduct of the public school as soon as the fine school building was completed. When the time came for selling the homes to the householders the volunteer organization of captains and householders was very helpful in inducing those who were then renting the properties to become the purchasers. All of the houses have been taken on an easy-payment purchase plan. The Housing Corporation no longer furnishes the funds for taking care of the public utilities, these now being supported out of taxes which the householders have levied upon themselves.

There was inaugurated a system of messages to be delivered by representatives of the local advisory committees to Negro audiences gathered on various occasions in different localities. These messages acquainted the people with the labor needs, opportunities and conditions. At the time the service was discontinued a series of economic surveys with special intensive survey of Norfolk, Va., were being planned for several cities in cooperation with local officials and citizens. These surveys were to include living conditions of Negro workers, such as housing surveys, sanitation, etc.

The constitution of the Negro Workers' Advisory Committee of Virginia is somewhat different from that of the other States, and shows so concretely how effectively cooperative connections were made with the State and local private organizations in existence that it is incorporated herewith the account of the work of Virginia instead of in an appendix:

CONSTITUTION OF THE NEGRO WORKERS' ADVISORY COMMITTEE OF VIRGINIA.

ARTICLE I. *Name.*—The name of this committee shall be the Negro Workers' Advisory Committee of Virginia.

ART. II. *Purpose.*—The purpose of this committee shall be to study, plan, and advise in a cooperative spirit and manner with employers of Negro labor, with Negro workers and with the United States Department of Labor in securing from Negro laborers greater production in industry and agriculture for winning the war through increasing regularity, application and efficiency, through increasing the morale of Negro workers, and through improving their general condition.

ART. III. *Membership.*—The membership of this committee shall be composed of not more than thirty persons—colored men and women of Virginia. At least five members shall be women. Seven members of this committee shall be chosen from the executive committee of the Negro Organization Society (Inc.), who shall be subject to reelection on the same terms of election as other members. The chairman of the Virginia Council of Defense, the Federal Director of the United States Employment Service, the chairman of the War Labor Board, and such other white citizens as may be appointed by the United States Department of Labor shall be cooperating members. Governor Westmoreland Davis shall be Honorary Chairman.

ART. IV. *Executive board.*—There shall be an executive board of nine chosen from the general committee. At least two members of the executive board shall be women, and three members shall be chosen from the central committee of the Negro Organization Society (Inc.), subject to the same terms of election as other members.

ART. V. *Appointments.*—The members of the committee and of the executive board shall upon recommendation be appointed by the Secretary of Labor, who shall also designate the chairman and the secretary. These officers shall serve for both the advisory committee and the executive board.

Upon the first appointment, one-third of the members of both the advisory committe and its executive board shall be appointed to serve until January 1, 1919; one-third to serve until June 1, 1919; and one-third to serve until January 1, 1920. Thereafter, one-third of the membership of the committee and its executive board shall be appointed every six months to serve for a term of six months. The chairman and secretary shall serve for periods of six months each, subject to reappointment. There shall be a treasurer appointed by the executive board. He shall be under bond for the faithful performance of such duties as the executive board may designate.

ART. VI. *Meetings.*—Section 1. The advisory committee shall meet at least once every six months and at such other times as the executive board may decide. Fifteen members shall constitute a quorum.

Sec. 2. The executive board shall meet at least once every other month and at such other times as the chairman and secretary shall decide, unless otherwise ordered by the board. Six members shall constitute a quorum. The chairman shall be required to call a meeting of the executive board upon a written request of five members of the advisory committee, of the board, or of both.

Sec. 3. The meeting place of the advisory committee and the executive board shall be the State Capitol unless otherwise ordered by the executive board and approved by the Department of Labor.

ART. VII. *By-laws.*—The executive board shall make such by-laws and rules for the conduct of business as seem best, subject to the approval of the advisory committee and the Department of Labor.

ART. VIII. *Powers of the executive board.*—The executive board shall transact all business, make plans, enter into agreements, and perform such other acts as may be necessary for carrying out the purpose of this committee. All such transactions, plans, agreements, or acts shall be subject to revision by the advisory committee and the United States Department of Labor, through its duly-authorized representatives.

ART. IX. *County committees.*—The executive board shall nominate for each county of the State having in their judgment a sufficient Negro population a county Negro workers' advisory committee of not more than eleven persons, at least two of whom must be women. This committee shall consist of one member from each magisterial district in the county and three members from the county at large, provided, however, that no county advisory committee shall consist of more than eleven members. Five members so nominated are to be appointed by the Department of Labor upon recommendation of the Negro Organization Society, (Inc.), or its central committee. A member of the respective county councils of defense and such other white citizens as may be selected by the Governor of Virginia, or his duly authorized representative, shall be cooperating members of the county advisory committee.

ART. X. *City committee.*—The executive board shall nominate for each city of the State having in their judgment a sufficient Negro population a city Negro workers' advisory committee of not more than twenty-five members, at least one-fifth of whom shall be women. A majority of the city advisory committee shall constitute a quorum for the transaction of business. Those nominated for this committee shall be appointed by the Department of Labor upon recommendation of the Negro Organization Society (Inc.), or its central committee.

Art. XI. *Neighborhood committees.*—Each district member of the county Negro workers' advisory committee shall appoint in his district a neighborhood committee consisting of one member for every five to fifteen families in the district. The district member of the county committee shall be chairman of this neighborhood committee and shall be held responsible for the work of the committee.

Art. XII. *Finances.*—Neither this organization, its executive board, nor the county or neighborhood committees, nor any of their executive boards shall have power or authority to incur expenses or make any financial agreements or contracts, which shall in any way obligate the State of Virginia, the United States Department of Labor, or the Negro Organization Society (Inc.) No debts shall be incurred by this committee or its executive board or by any county or neighborhood committees or their respective executive boards unless previously provided for. The treasurer of this committee shall keep account of receipts and expenditures and he shall keep any funds intrusted to him deposited in such banks or trust companies as the executive board shall decide.

Art. XIII. *Amendments.*—Amendments may be made to this constitution by two-thirds vote at a regular and duly called meeting of this committee, provided such amendment shall have been previously approved by the governor of Virginia, or his duly authorized representative, and the United States Department of Labor and the Negro Organization Society (Inc).

CHAPTER XIX.

NEGRO WOMEN IN INDUSTRY.

SUMMARY OF REPORTS MADE BY MRS. HELEN B. IRVIN, SPECIAL AGENT OF THE WOMEN'S BUREAU IN 1918–19.

Desiring to give recognition to all major questions affecting women in industry and keeping in mind the declared purpose of the United States Department of Labor "to foster, promote, and develop the welfare of wage earners of the United States," the Women's Bureau, early in its career as the Woman in Industry Service, made provision to include in its program a study of the problems of Negro women in industry. The summary of data here given was secured from several industrial centers where typical conditions were known to prevail during visits made within the seven months beginning December 1, 1918, and ending June 30, 1919.

This summary is by no means extensive. One hundred and fifty-two plants, employing more than 21,000 Negro workers, were visited, and the figures and statements here presented cover recent phases and developments in this industrial situation.

The plants and industries visited were located in Illinois, Ohio, and Missouri, and in portions of New Jersey, Pennsylvania, and Virginia. In a number of cases recommendations were made for the improvement of conditions. Wherever subsequent information could be obtained showing that action had followed these recommendations and some instructive experience resulted a statement has been included in this summary.

INDUSTRIAL OPPORTUNITIES FOR NEGRO WOMEN.

The total number of Negroes 10 years of age and over who were gainfully employed in 1910 as reported by the Thirteenth Census was 5,192,535; of these, 3,178,554 were male workers and 2,013,981 were female workers. Of the female workers, 1,051,137 were included in agriculture, forestry, and animal husbandry. Only 8,313 were listed in trade and transportation occupations, and 67,967 in manufacturing and mechanical pursuits.[1]

While these figures include women in all sections of the country, of wide range of training, and of all ages above 10 years, it is reported that, on an average, Negro women in industry are between 16 and 30 years of age. With the great labor shortage during the war, especially in northern industries, colored women had the opportunity to enter industrial pursuits never opened to them before. For the country as a whole there are at present no available figures to show the full extent to which they embraced the opportunities. The figures included below, however, are so typical as to give a good indication for the territory covered. As a result of recent migration in the North, these women were frequently new to urban life and to the factory type of community. They were, therefore, largely in process of adjustment to unaccustomed conditions, climatic, social, occupational, and economic.

---

[1] Department of Commerce, Bureau of the Census, Negro Population 1790–1915. General Tables Nos. 17 and 19.

MACHINE OPERATORS MAKING BEDSPRING WEBBING.

The great need for workers to replace men drafted for Army service brought women into occupations not heretofore considered within the range of their possible activities. Negro women shared to some extent these new fields. In response to the industrial demand, large numbers dropped their accustomed tasks in the home and in domestic service to take up the newer, more attractive work of supplying the need of the fighting world for the products of industry. In visits to 152 typical plants employing Negro women it was found that they were working at many different processes and under very different working conditions. Table VII which follows, gives an outline of the kind of work done by the women and the industries in which they were employed:

TABLE VII.—*Industrial occupations of 21,547 Negro women in (approximately) 75 specific processes, at 152 plants, during the period Dec. 1, 1918, to June 30, 1919.*

Number of plants inspected.	Product.	Processes at which women were employed.	Number of women employed, each specified process.
1	Bed springs	Assembling, miscellaneous	4
		Machine operating	16
2	Brooms, brushes	Grading broom corn, binding bristles.	190
5	Canned foods	Pitting, packing, crystallizing, and canning fruits and vegetables.	311
26	Clothing (men's and women's)	Cutting	2
		Draping	5
		Hand finishing	11
		Machine sewing	632
4	Cotton mills (cordage, waste, mops)	Feeding and tending machines	190
		Sorting cotton	100
31	Department and other stores	Elevator operators	110
		Saleswomen	3
		Stock girls, maids	228
		Wrappers	37
4	Furniture	Operating lathes	7
		Polishing desks, pianos	25
1	Glassware	Making blown glass	102
		Matron, timekeeper	2
7	Hardware	Miscellaneous machine operating punch and drill presses soldering, welding.	360
4	Hosiery and knit goods	Finishing knitted garments	38
		Operating knitting machines	692
6	Laundries	Steam and dry cleaning	11
		Washing and ironing by power machinery.	146
3	Leather goods	Grading, cleaning and curing, tanning hides.	130
5	Meats and meat products (stockyards, abattoirs).	Cleaning and curing offal	2,990
		Preparing, curing, and canning meats.	117
		Testing hides	37
		Time keeping	2
		Trimming and cleaning viscera	136
2	Munitions	Loading shells	499
16	Office work (Government work, mail-order houses).	Billing machines and addressograph operators.	331
		Card filing, clerking	2,705
		Expert investigating	7
		Packing and shipping goods	182
		Skilled field work (lectures, etc.)	8
		Switchboard operating	2
		Typists, stenographers, bookkeepers	2,303
4	Rubber goods	Making and vulcanizing motor tires, tubes, rubber toys, etc.	114
16	Tobacco	Making cigars	48
		Preparing snuff and chewing tobacco.	2,373
		Stemming	5,965
		Weighing and inspecting	2
12	Transportation	Cleaning and repairing automobiles	215
		Flagging trains	18
		Salvaging from railroad wreckage	84
3	War apparatus (gas masks, aeroplane sails, balloons).	Power-machine stitching	57
	Total		21,547

It will be seen from a study of this table that the two industries employing the greatest number of Negro women were the meat-packing industry, where 3,282 were employed in the stockyards and abattoirs, and the tobacco industry, where 5,965 were employed at stemming tobacco, and 2,373 in the preparation of chewing tobacco and of snuff.

Another very large group were doing office work, 5,538 being employed in 16 offices. The other occupations ranged from the simple work of sorting and packing to the operation of various machines requiring skill and dexterity. Some of these occupations, such as loading shells, operating lathes, cleaning and repairing automobiles, flagging trains, and salvaging from railroad wreckage, were new to all women. On the greater number of processes, however, white women had been employed many years before Negro women were taken on.

During the war the employment of large numbers of women at new tasks in munitions plants and other war industries led to a shortage of labor in the textile and garment factories, which had long been great employers of women. As a result many textile and garment manufacturers, being quite unable to secure the requisite number of white workers for their plants, accepted and even appealed to Negro girls and women to relieve the situation. The work of 1,670 girls and women in textile and garment trades was carefully observed. Several thousand others were known to be similarly employed.

In several arsenals and munition plants groups of Negro women were found mixing chemicals, loading shells, making gas masks, stitching wings for aeroplanes, and engaging in similar processes requiring great care, skillful fingers, patriotism, and courage. Most of these industries were housed in modern fireproof buildings, well ventilated to carry off the poisonous fumes, asbestos partitioned to prevent the spread of flames, and well equipped with hose, fire escapes, and first-aid apparatus for use in the occasional accidents that appear to be unavoidable in such places.

The 499 munition makers were found to be giving satisfaction as a whole, and in some instances were reported to respond more readily than others for doing the heavy and dangerous portions of the work. They were proud of their unusual tasks and of their uniforms, and seem to have appreciated the working day shorter than household hours in domestic and personal service.

In abattoirs, stockyards, and tanneries Negro women were engaged at different times in all processes except the actual butchering and inspecting of meats. They trimmed, sorted, and graded different portions of the carcasses; separated and cleaned the viscera; prepared, cured, and canned the meats; and graded, cleaned, cured, and tanned the hides for making articles of leather.

In Government clothing factories and in private establishments on Government contracts they made overalls, army shirts, and dungarees in large numbers. In other factories they made bolts, nuts, rivets, screws, motor accessories, and metal buckets. In rubber plants they made automobile tires, tubes, parts of rubber boots, shoe heels, toys, and hospital necessities, such as rubber gloves, pads, and hot-water bottles. In transportation service they cleaned cars, acted as switch-

NEGRO WOMEN IRONERS IN LAUNDRY ESTABLISHMENT. (NOTE THE VENTILATING HOOD.)

men and flagmen, mended roadbeds, salvaged small parts of engines and coaches from wreckage, painted and made simple repairs on automobiles, and occasionally acted as chauffeurs.

Power-laundry work has furnished the opportunity for many Negro girls and women to earn a livelihood. In considerable numbers they have followed into the factory their former occupation of laundering clothing. Under good factory conditions this permits of escape from the more undesirable conditions of the household laundry service. Because of the difficulties and dangers of the work, and because of the traditional linking of Negro women to such tasks, there has been in most places little objection to them or color discrimination against them in laundries. They have learned, consequently, to operate all kinds of power-laundry machinery; to wash, iron, steam or dry clean garments of all sorts, as well as to do the hand finishing that is still in considerable demand.

Many of these industries being essential in peace times, it is probable that large numbers of the Negro women who were drawn into them during the war emergency, and have made good, will find permanent occupations at more desirable work than heretofore.

In these industries Negro women usually fell heir to the less desirable occupations or processes. As a whole, however, they stuck to these jobs and many won advancement to higher places in that way. Many are still to be found spinning coarse yarn; knitting gloves, stockings, and underwear of cheap grades; making lingerie, fine waists, silk and woolen dresses, coats, caps, overalls, and men's shirts.

The 8,388 tobacco workers observed in the factories visited were found chiefly in southern or border-line States, and, with the exception of two groups, are working under most objectionable, insanitary conditions. Nearly 6,000 of these young, unskilled girls, work in stemmeries, where they prepare the stemmed tobacco for chewing, cigar making, snuff, and cigarettes. Very few Negro girls are found at the more skilled processes, such as making cigars. For this work one employment manager insisted upon hiring only pretty types, of rather foreign appearance, "in order that they may be regarded by patrons as Cuban, South American, or Spanish." Two women who were employed as weighers or inspectors were found to be both quick and accurate in their judgment, and are paving the way for others.

In hotels many Negro women performed the services of cooks, dishwashers, waitresses, maids, elevator operators, and even bell girls. These latter were afterward quite generally replaced by boys and men, the girls being unable to handle most of the luggage of patrons. The wages of maids and waitresses were usually low, the workers being largely dependent upon "tips."

Elevator girls were operating both in hotels and in department stores as well as in many office buildings. They worked on alternate long and short "shifts," with brief rest periods, and carried passengers or freight as required. However, they were not usually compelled to lift packages into or out of their cars. Not only have these girls succeeded as elevator operators, but also as maids, stock girls, bundle wrappers, and even, where given the opportunity, as saleswomen. Several employers expressed a marked preference for Negro stock girls, for reason that a greater variety of service might be demanded of them.   For instance, in some stores they came to work 15 minutes before schedule time in order to polish mirrors and display cases.

Careful observation showed that bundle wrappers working in sight of customers of stores were often of types whose racial identity was doubtful, while those behind the screens, as in packing and shipping departments, were more distinctly negroid in complexion. Three saleswomen of discernible Negro blood were of good appearance and showed keen intelligence about their work.   Three or four quick and clever stock girls were found acting as sales assistants.

Excepting Government appointees, of whom varying numbers have held positions under civil-service regulations since the period of reconstruction following the Civil War, comparatively few Negro women were employed at office work until 1917.   The general spur to industry consequent upon America's participation in the war, the shifting of workers from home and farm to office, factory, and battlefield made opportunities for greater numbers at clerical tasks than ever before.   In this emergency several thousand Negro women found opportunities to play their part.   The total of 5,538 found doing office work qualified in the offices of shops, of mail-order and other business houses, as typists, stenographers, and bookkeepers, 2,303 were observed at this work.   There were 2,705 filing clerks, 331 billing and addressograph operators, and 182 packing and shipping clerks.   These included, of course, forewomen and supervisors of the various groups of workers.   Clerical work was being done for the Government under civil-service and special classification.   Also, there were 15 special investigators and lecturers and 2 telephone switchboard operators.

A majority of these clerical workers, both in general commercial and industrial plants and in Government service, were given temporary appointments under the war emergency.   Many of them were being released after the armistice to make way for discharged soldiers or because need for their services no longer existed.   Others were frankly told that such positions as remained available were intended for white workers, and that they had been used merely because no others could at that time be obtained.   In known instances, however, Negro girls and women acquitted themselves in so satisfactory a manner that they have been retained, these having made permanent places for themselves.   Also, a number of instances of individual success and achievement are known to have been rewarded by promotion and by assurance of continuance during satisfactory service.

The signing of the armistice, bringing about a gradual cessation of war industries or a change in factory processes and products, probably meant the permanent dismissal of many of these Negro women industrial workers.   Some have been provided for in the new plans of their employers and others have returned to their prewar occupations.   Subsequent study is in progress to ascertain to what extent these Negro women have found a permanent foothold in these industrial occupations.

NEGRO WOMEN AT WORK AS ENTRY CLERKS IN A MAIL-ORDER HOUSE.

CONDITIONS OF EMPLOYMENT.

In individual plants conditions were found to vary from the least desirable to the most satisfactory, as judged by modern industrial standards. Outstanding examples of these differences are to be found particularly in types of factory work usually denoted as "women's trades," such as textile, clothing, and tobacco industries. On the whole, the working conditions where Negro women were employed along with white women the conditions appeared to be similar. A few typical cases will illustrate the situation.

In a hoisery mill employing Negro women no provision was made for first aid, although slight accidents are frequent. Other facilities for the comfort of the workers were at a minimum. The plant had no lunchroom or lockers. There were but two toilets and two sinks, and one separate faucet with a tin cup attached supplied the drinking water for the entire group. There was neither soap nor warm water for washing the hands, although the workers were expected to keep the white hosiery quite free of any soiling. They were taxed a few cents for each soiled spot found by the inspector.

On the other hand, another establishment, manufacturing men's shirts, offered thoroughly desirable working conditions with adequate facilities for the comfort of its employees. Each unit, consisting of 140 to 200 girls, was furnished with an instructor for processes that were new, whether carried on by hand or by power machine. The shops were well lighted and heated and were fitted with modern machinery that runs with little noise and gives to the operators protection from accident. A small dispensary and first-aid room, with a nurse, were available. There was an excellent lunch room, with food furnished at cost. There were lockers, clean and adequate toilets, and sinks with soap and sanitary towels. All workers started with the same basic wage, with increases to more highly paid piecework as rapidly as their skill permitted.

Good and bad conditions were found also among industries heretofore carried on entirely by men. For instance, a plant manufacturing buckets and other sheet-metal products was very poorly heated, lighted, and ventilated. Its uneven cement floor held pools of water that had overflowed from the cooling tanks. Generously spilled paint and solder caused an uncertain footing in the dim aisles.

One room, about 9 by 12 feet, with a single toilet in the corner and with hooks above two benches along the walls, furnished the only arrangements for women to change street clothing and working apparel and for the storage of coats and skirts of changed garments. There being no lockers, garments of workers were frequently reported as lost from the hooks. Two sinks just outside the door of this room were supplied merely with cold water, and only roller towels were furnished.

Under these conditions two groups of 35 Negro women each worked on alternate day and night shifts. One group worked from 7 p. m. until 5 a. m., with a half hour at midnight for lunch. Because of the extreme suburban location of this plant and the inconvenience to cars these employees were obliged to walk about half mile across an unpaved, poorly lighted, wind-swept area which was unpleasant even on a clear winter midday, not to mention inclement weather.

A group of young Negro women, selected and sent by the local United States Employment office in response to an urgent appeal from the woman proprietor, left this factory in a body on their first day because of the abusive language of a foreman in response to their protest against the conditions under which they were expected to work.

In marked contrast to these conditions were those found in an immense plant which was making bolts, nuts, small parts of motors, and other machine-shop products. The several hundred women employees were native-born white, Negro, and foreign-born of several nationalities. The workrooms of this factory were light and clean, neither unduly noisy nor overcrowded. The punch and drill presses were provided with guards to reduce the number of accidents. The Negro women wore caps and overalls and were directed by a Negro forewoman. The plant was adequately equipped with toilets, washrooms, and lockers. There was a plain but clean lunchroom, a dispensary, with first-aid and visiting-nurse service without charge. There was also a company store where employees could purchase uniforms, other plain clothing, and a few necessary foodstuffs at wholesale rates. A training school offered certain instruction during a limited number of hours each working week. There was apparently no special arrangements made because of race, except that the colored women worked in a group to themselves and were superintended by a Negro forewoman.

Realizing that the opinion of their employers would seriously affect the future of Negro women in industry, an attempt was made to secure the opinions of superintendents or other officials dealing with Negro women in these plants. Of 34 employers who expressed a definite opinion on this subject, 14 said that they found the work of Negro women as satisfactory as other women workers, and 3 found their work better than that of the white women they were working with or had displaced. Of the 17 employers who felt that the work of Negro women did not compare satisfactorily with that of the white women, 7 reported that irregularity of attendance was the main cause for dissatisfaction, and 7 others felt that the output of Negro women was less because they were slower workers.

INDUSTRIAL TRAINING.

The chief of the problems of industrial training is presented by the very obvious need for a more carefully thought-out plan of education for Negro women, who are comparatively new to industry and who have no adequate standards upon which to base their estimate of their own worth or the requirements of their occupations.

If private and public facilities were to be generally opened to Negro women for their education there would not fail to be a very general increase in the efficiency of Negro women in industry. This is not education in the usually accepted sense, though an impartial enforcement of the school attendance law will improve economic conditions for future groups of workers. It is training for efficiency, with its contributing factors of personal hygiene, industrial sense, increasing skill, and realization of contractual obligation. It is the development of industrial consciousness through the fostering of pride in achievement, through increasing personal and family thrift and through encouraging an attitude of constancy toward a given task or locality. This type of education is essential in "training the worker on the job."

As is the case with any group new to a situation, Negro women on entering industry have need of patient, careful training in all processes required of them and in the use of all machinery employed in the specific work assigned to them. Such training plus the opportunity to advance individually or in groups, as their increasing skill may warrant, has been found profitable by most of the employers who are awake to the possibilities of Negro women as workers. Eighty per cent of the employers interviewed who had given a trial to the training-plus-opportunity method reported little or no difficulty with these workers, while 30 per cent expressed a preference for Negro women because of their cheerfulness, willingness, and loyalty in response to fair treatment.

One employer who had instituted these courses said: "We are getting all we hoped for and more." In this plant the girls were doing clerical work. Each girl was given three days' special training before being put to work. Up to the time of the visit (1919) their work was so satisfactory that a large number were employed. The management said that it had found that Negro girls did just as good clerical work as white girls as soon as the "breaking-in" training had been given.

In another plant, where a "superintendent of service" was detailed to superintend group and individual training for work on small machine products, it was reported that there was no difference between the work or attendance of the native-born white, Negro, and and foreign-born women workers. This plant showed in the kind of women employed and the atmosphere of the workroom the excellent results of the absolutely equal chance given to all workers. In other plants training was more haphazard, being given by the forewoman and sometimes by fellow workers. It was from such establishments that the greater number of complaints of inefficiency and slowness came.

In addition to courses of training supplied by the employer within his plant and which are limited to the actual processes in use in his plant, there were found some opportunities for Negro women in the public schools, through continuation classes or night schools.

In one locality a plan of cooperation for such extension work between the vocational bureau of the public schools and a privately controlled industrial school was feasible. The school in question had already launched several courses designed to interest the young working girls of that community. The principal was quite willing to extend the opportunity to Negro women workers, making such course as practically attractive as the school facilities would permit. At the time this school was offering courses of interest to housemaids, cafeteria workers, butchers, core makers, motor mechanics, and various sorts of garment workers, including makers of overalls, shirts, and women's clothing.

Possibilities for decent, sane, healthful recreation for the average Negro working girl and woman being in many communities distressingly inadequate, this phase of educational activity is very essential to efficiency. It appeared wise to attempt to arouse interest in this matter wherever the situation seemed urgently to warrant it.

As an instance of what can be done, a community center organization which had previously taken no heed of the 300 to 400 colored girls at work in a local factory was persuaded to provide for them a weekly meeting place and a leader of games and athletics. The principal of a Negro school was induced to appeal to the school authorities to include in their plan for a new building some provision for a joint assembly room and gymnasium. Much to the principal's surprise the appeal met a favorable reception, and the people of the little community are now watching the erection of their building with this addition.

Several recreational clubs of different sorts have been organized in churches, and a certain war service has given excellent and valuable assistance in this respect, following most willingly any lead or suggestion that might be given.

A very important part of the work which was done by the Women's Bureau in connection with Negro women was the educational talks explaining to various groups interested in this subject the standards and policies that should attain in establishments employing women and girls.

In addition to the courses of training which could be made available for Negro workers in the private or public schools, there could be a most valuable educational stimulus and training given in the various leagues and clubs of industrial women workers which are organized in different communities.

METHODS OF SUPERVISION.

If the Negro woman is to keep and increase her hold in industrial activities of the country, in addition to special training to fit her for the work, she will need the cooperation of employers who understand the special problems attending her employment, and who will make adjustments and establish policies accordingly. Various methods of shop management in plants employing Negro and white workers together were noted during this survey, and on the basis of successful experiments that were observed recommendations were made for the improvement of conditions in other localities.

In one northern community which had recently been subjected to a large influx of Negroes one well-known firm had already put into operation a plan of work for them on equal pay and conditions as other workers. The results were not only satisfactory but were promising of most desirable further development. The workers were making good in every department. The largest numbers naturally were found in sections where mainly manual operations were required. Besides the many operators on punch and drill presses there were several forewomen, five typists, two or three clerks, two messengers, two elevator operators, a first-aid assistant, a postwoman, and a woman chauffeur. With this particular firm as a successful example three others were persuaded to give their Negro workers similar opportunity.

Negro women supervisors of units of workers of their own kind were giving results. One very successful instance of such supervision can be used as an example of what might be accomplished through the more general adoption of the plan. This unit of approximately 200 girls in a large mail-order house had worked for about a year under the supervision of an intelligent Negro woman. The work of these girls consisted of all office processes, such as bookkeeping, stenographic work, typewriting, and operating office appliances as well as packing and preparing goods for shipment.

These workers were not only supervised but were also trained and instructed by Negro forewomen. The unit had a slogan, "Make good 100 per cent." So successful had been the work of this group that shortly after their dismissal by a new, unsympathetic superintendent, they were reinstated and their number augmented, because their work was so satisfactory in relation to the larger work of the entire plant.

Although there was a number of examples found of a carefully thought out policy in the employment of Negro women, there were complaints of discrimination made by these women too serious and frequent to be ignored. If a group of women persistently believes that they are given the lowest wages, the most disagreeable work, the poorest material, and that they will be the first to be laid off, whether or not the facts fully warrant their beliefs, they will hardy put their best efforts into the improvement of their work.

SUMMARY AND CONCLUSION.

From the foregoing account it would seem that the Negro women have taken an increasingly important place in industrial activities, largely as a result of labor shortage during the war. They increased in numbers in meat packing, in the tobacco industry and power laundries, and entered largely into textile and garment factories, munitions plants, and into clerical positions.

The conditions of the places of work varied from excellent to very poor, appearing to be similar to those surrounding white women where the two were working together. The Negro women workers need special attention to their industrial training and opportunities for community adjustment. Where employers have tried to do this they found it profitable. Special supervision, especially by persons of their own race, has proven effective.

So far as the situation may be regarded as peculiar to the Negro woman it may be said that she has been accepted, in the main, as an experiment; her admittance to a given occupation or plant has been conditioned upon no other workers being available, and her continuance frequently hinged upon the same. She was usually given the less desirable jobs. The Negro woman worker being new to industry has to learn its lessons of routine and regularity; the attitude both of the employer and of other workers toward Negro women workers was one of uncertainty.

CHAPTER XX.

RECOMMENDATIONS ON SCOPE OF DEPARTMENTAL AUTHORITY.

From time to time the Director of Negro Economics submitted reports and memoranda to the Secretary of Labor showing the propaganda which it was attempted to establish among Negro wage earners. Such a memorandum, with supporting documents and newspaper clippings and exhibits, were submitted to the Secretary about a month before the series of riots in Chicago, Ill., Omaha, Nebr., Washington, D. C., and other places in the summer of 1919. In this memorandum there were analyzed the three schools of opinion and activities in the adjustment of Negro life, namely, the very radical I. W. W. group, the aggressive abolitionist group, and the conciliatory group. In the course of this memorandum, dated July 8, 1919, there occurred the following statements:

This state of opinion in the Negro world is especially important with reference to the labor conditions in the States of Pennsylvania, Ohio, Illinois, Michigan, and points in New Jersey, Indiana, Nebraska, Iowa, and Kansas. To this territory thousands of Negroes have migrated and are still moving. They are coming into employments very much more highly paid than those they left in the South. They are badly housed in most cases, rather coolly received by the white workers and populace, segregated into "ghettos" in the larger industrial centers. They are little adjusted to the highly organized northern life into which they have come from more backward communities in the South. The white workers in many localities in this territory have looked with apprehension upon their settlement, at the present time there being considerable friction in points like Toledo, Ohio, Chicago, Ill., and Omaha, Nebr. The occurrences at Philadelphia, East St. Louis, and Chester, Pa., within the last two years are only indications of what may easily take place in other places. * * * The returning Negro soldiers are also going in large numbers to these centers.

Their discontent, growing out of previous conditions and present maladjustment in their new surroundings, their desire for American rights, their resentment against unjust discrimination and other practices against them make them a very ripe field for critical developments of unrest, friction, and disturbances—dangers not only to the peace of labor conditions but also to the welfare of themselves, the community, and the Nation. Suspicions of white workers at the present time in several places make outbreaks easily possible. * * *

In all this territory there is very little, if any, well-organized and well-directed machinery for assisting Negroes in getting into touch with the employment offices and in getting located and adjusted in their new environment. Thousands of them are coming to places like Chicago and Detroit with no direction whatever. They will listen to counsel and guidance from Federal agents as from no others.

It has been clearly demonstrated that our supervisors, working under the United States Employment Service, with the development of Negro workers' advisory committees in these places, can have the most far-reaching effect upon these workers.

During the trying days of the Chicago riots the Director of Negro Economics went to Chicago and investigated the situation on the ground and on August 27, 1919, he made a full report of the Chicago situation to the Secretary of Labor, outlining the underlying labor causes in relation to white employers, white workmen, Negro workmen, housing, political, and other conditions. This report was supported with a mass of testimony, newspaper clippings, and other data. The director also visited and reported upon the feeling between white and colored workers in St. Louis, Mo., Detroit and Flint, Mich., Cleveland, Ohio, and several other places. Testimony and evidence were also gathered from Sumter and Columbia, S. C., Birmingham, Ala., New York, N. Y., Jacksonville, Fla., and Montgomery, Ala., and from this testimony the director said, as a preface to the following recommendations (see pp. 26–31):

I am led to believe that the racial tension is so widespread as to be, in fact, a matter of national concern calling for some attention from the National Government.

He therefore made the following recommendations which were transmitted by the Assistant Secretary of Labor and approved by the Secretary of Labor September 29, 1919:

This report of racial friction, together with my previous memorandum on racial unrest, submitted July 8, 1919, shows imperative need of some forward steps. When the Secretary of Labor, furthering the effectiveness of his office, created the position of Director of Negro Economics there was latently established a means of exchange of information and of cooperation between this department and other departments of government, both State and Federal, through which a large, National constructive program for bettering the living and working conditions of Negro workers and improving their relations with white workers and white employers may be outlined and put into operation. The authority of the Secretary to establish such cooperation between this department and other departments is given in the organic act as follows:

"Said Secretary [of Labor] shall also have authority to call upon other departments of the Government for statistical data and the results obtained by them; and said Secretary of Labor may collate, arrange, and publish such statistical information obtained in such manner as to him may seem wise." (Sec. 4 of the organic act creating the Department of Labor.)

Section 10 of the organic act directed the Secretary to report to Congress a plan for coordination of the activities, duties, and powers of his office with those of other offices so far as they relate to labor. January 9, 1917, the Secretary of Labor reported such a plan to Congress with a bill to establish such cooperation and coordination of activities, powers, and duties. (See H. Doc. No. 1906, 64th Cong. 2d sess.) Apparently this bill was never enacted into law.

However, the Director of Negro Economics has been acting under the authority of the Secretary given in section 4 of the organic act quoted above so far as cooperation could be obtained with other departments in obtaining and furnishing information for the advice of the department. In addition to effective cooperation of an advisory nature which has been established with the several bureaus and divisions of the Department of Labor, special steps for cooperation with other branches of the Federal Government and with some of the State governments have been successfully undertaken. Special mention may be made of such cooperative effort with the State Councils of National Defense during the war, with the United States Public Health Service, and the War Risk Insurance Bureau of the Treasury Department, and with Col. Woods's office (Special Assistant to the Secretary of War), and with some of the demonstration agents of the Department of Agriculture.

Based upon this past experience and the authority and powers of the Secretary of Labor for calling upon other branches of the Government for information affecting wage earners, I respectfully recommend:

1. That the office of the Secretary of Labor, by virtue of the aforesaid authority, either through the Division of Negro Economics, or otherwise, as seems best, take steps through the executive of each department, or chiefs of bureaus or commissions or boards, (a) to develop cooperation for securing statistical data on labor matters from other departments, such data to be collated, arranged, and published with reference to Negro workers and their relations to white workers and white employers; (b) to work out plans for practical cooperation of the office of the Secretary of Labor with such other branches of the executive department of the Government as deals with questions of labor, such plans to be similar to those already started with the Public Health Service, the Bureau of War Risk Insurance of the Treasury Department, and the office of Col. Woods, of the War Department.

2. That the Negro Workers' Advisory Committees already established be utilized for such cooperative service with other departments of the Government for such steps as may be effective in removing the conditions now causing racial unrest and friction,

as it seems to me that some of the causes can be effectively removed by cooperative efforts of the agencies of the Federal Government along the following lines: (*a*) Publicity and educational campaigns on the training of Negro workers, both shop training and unskilled training; (*b*) improvement of the housing of Negro workers; (*c*) methods of encouraging thrift; (*d*) improvement of farm labor conditions and methods of labor management; (*f*) educational efficiency campaigns on promptness, regularity, full-time work, etc., utilizing Negro newspapers, associations, agencies, and public speakers; and (*g*) enlistment of active help of white employers and organizations of white workers.

3. That through the cooperation of the other agencies of the Federal Government some plan for the investigation of Negro affairs and race relations in as many localities as possible be undertaken as a means of having information and advice to improve conditions and race relations.

4. That steps be taken with appropriate departments of State governments similar to those already established in North Carolina, Ohio, and Illinois.

APPENDIX I.

LABOR AND VICTORY.

[An address prepared and sent out for use in Fourth of July celebrations, 1918. About 2,000 copies were distributed and it is estimated that it was heard by more than 1,000,000 Negroes.]

This is a world struggle for democracy, and win it we must.

How can we win it? There is but one way. Everyone—man, woman, and child, be he a millionaire or a day laborer—must do his level best at his work, wherever he may be, whether on the farm, at the docks, in the machine shop, in the mill, at the White House in Washington, in the kitchen, in the home, or in the trenches. Even wealthy society women in our own country are giving up their luxuries, children are giving up their candy, that the children of Europe may have bread.

To win this war our soldiers must go to France and fight; but they can not fight unless they have guns and ammunition. They can not fight unless they have clothing and shoes, and tents, and plenty of food. They can not have these things unless there are ships to carry them to France. We must have ships and more ships. We must build steel ships; we must build wooden ships; we must build concrete ships, to hurry our men and war supplies to the front. Thoughtful men and women, how can our soldiers have clothing and shoes and food? How can we have ships to carry our boys to France? There is but one way. Every man, and every child and woman, must work and save, to furnish food, to make clothing and shoes, to make guns and ammunition, and to build ships. And do not forget that any person, black or white, who does not work hard, who lags in any way, who fails to buy a Liberty bond, or a War Savings stamp if he can, is against his country and is, therefore, our bitter enemy.

I am happy to say that the majority of our men and women are working like all other good Americans to make their labor win the war. Only a few weeks ago the world's record for driving rivets in building steel ships was broken by Charles Knight, a Negro workman at Sparrows Point, Md. In one nine-hour day he drove 4,875 three-quarter inch rivets in the hull of a steel ship. The newspapers of the country have lauded him for his work. The British Government sent him a prize of $125. Again, many of our men and women are making records as workers in the steel mills, in the coal mines, on the railroads, and on the farms. Our thoughtful, interested cooks and other helpers in the kitchen are really doing service at the front, by saving all the food they can. The newspapers and journals of the country, managed and edited by thoughtful men and women, are creating sentiment that will do much toward winning the war. For instance, the Albany (Ga.) Herald, a newspaper edited by Southern white men, advised and suggested to ladies of the city who offered to make and present to the city a service flag, that a service flag for Albany would not be complete unless there were placed in its field a star not only for every white soldier or sailor who has enlisted from Albany but a

137

star for every·Albanian, white or black.   The first employee of this newspaper to join the National Army was a Negro, and the first star on the Herald's service flag is his star.

Negroes are being asked in every city, town, and rural district to join in this work of winning this war.   We, like other folk, are having an unusual chance to work and save our country.   Let every one of us be wide awake, and make the most of this opportunity.   Let him bear in mind that every time he makes good on his job, he helps his country and the race.   Let him also remember that every time a Negro falls down on his job, he pulls down his country and the entire race, and thus makes winning the war less possible.

A few months ago a friend printed a card to help the Negro workmen in factories and shops.   The card read something like this:

WHY HE FAILED.

He did not report on time;
He watched the clock;
He loafed when the boss was not looking;
He stayed out with the boys all night;
He said, "I forgot;"
He did not show up on Monday, and
He wanted a holiday every Saturday;
He lied when asked for the truth.

There is still another thing we ought to think about, if we are to make the most of these opportunities for saving our country.   These are times of great demands and great prosperity.   Wages are high. Everybody who will work can get work.   Many who are working now are making more money than they ever made.   Many of our families who have men in the Army are now getting from Uncle Sam more cash money than they ever had at any one time before.   What then is the wise thing for us to do now?   In the words of the proverbs of Solomon: "Go to the ant, thou sluggard; consider her ways and be wise.   She layeth up her store in summer."   Now is the time to work every day we can.   Now is the time to work every hour we can.   Now is the time to make and save every dollar we can.   Now is the time to buy every Liberty bond we can, and every War Savings stamp that we can, in order that our country may have that liberty for which she is fighting.   The Negro has fought like a man in the battles from Bunker Hill to San Juan Hill.   He has died to keep the American colors flying.   Those left behind did their duty like soldiers, and to-day there are hundreds of black boys at the front in France laying down their very lives for their country, for you and for me. Will you, because of your refusal to work six days in every week, or because of your failure to save as much food as you can, or because of any lack of interest whatever on your part, have to answer to our boys on their return, maimed in battle or even to men who never return?   We are our brothers' keepers; we, too, are soldiers on duty, and in our hands rests the destiny of our country and our fellow men America needs, expects, and asks every man to do his duty.

APPENDIX II.

CONSTITUTION OF THE NEGRO WORKERS' ADVISORY COMMITTEE OF NORTH CAROLINA.

ARTICLE I. *Name.*—The name of this committee shall be the Negro Workers' Advisory Committee of North Carolina.

ART. II. *Purpose.*—The purpose of this committee shall be to study, plan, and advise in a cooperative spirit and manner with employees of Negro labor, with Negro workers, and with the United States Department of Labor in securing from Negro laborers greater production in industry and agriculture for winning the war through increasing regularity, application, and efficiency, through increasing the morale of Negro workers, and through improving their general conditions.

ART. III. *Membership.*—The membership of this committee shall be composed of not more than 30 persons, colored men and women of North Carolina. At least five members shall be women. The chairman of the North Carolina Council of Defense, the Federal director of the United States Employment Service, and the State agent of rural schools shall be cooperating members. The governor shall be honorary chairman.

ART. IV. *Executive board.*—There shall be an executive board of nine chosen from the general committee. At least two members of the executive board shall be women.

ART. V. *Appointments.*—The members of the committee and of the executive board shall, upon recommendation, be appointed by the Secretary of Labor, who shall also designate the chairman and the secretary. These officers shall serve for both the advisory committee and the executive board.

Upon the first appointment one-third of the members of both the advisory committee and its executive board shall be appointed to serve until January 1, 1919; one-third to serve until June 1, 1919; and one-third to serve until January 1, 1920. Thereafter one-third of the membership of the committee and its executive board shall be appointed every six months to serve for a term of six months. The chairman and secretary shall serve for periods of six months each, subject to reappointment.

ART. VI. *Meetings.*—Section 1. The advisory committee shall meet at least once every six months and at such other times as the executive board may decide. Fifteen members shall constitute a quorum.

Sec. 2. The executive board shall meet at least once every other month and at such other times as the chairman and secretary shall decide, unless otherwise ordered by the board. Six members shall constitute a quorum. The chairman shall be required to call the meeting of the executive board upon the written request of five members.

Sec. 3. The meeting place of the advisory committee and the executive board shall be the State Capitol, unless otherwise ordered by the executive board and approved by the Department of Labor.

ART. VII. *By-laws.*—The executive board shall make such by-laws and rules for the conduct of business as seem best, subject to the approval of the advisory committee, and the Department of Labor.

ART. VIII. *Powers of the executive board.*—The executive board shall transact all business, make plans, enter into agreements, and form such other acts as may be necessary for carrying out the purpose of this committee. All such transactions, plans, agreements, or acts shall be subject to revision by the advisory committee and the United States Department of Labor, through its duly authorized representatives.

ART. IX. *County committees.*—The executive board shall nominate for each county of the State having in their judgment a sufficient Negro population a county Negro workers' advisory committee of not more than 11 persons. These persons so nominated are to be appointed by the Department of Labor upon recommendation of the county council of defense of their respective counties. The chairmen of the respective county councils of defense and such other white citizens as may be selected by the Department of Labor shall be cooperating members of the county advisory committee.

ART. X. *District committees.*—The county advisory committee may be authorized by the State committee to form district advisory committees for localities in their respective counties where the Negro population and local labor problems justify such district advisory committees.

ART. XI. *Finances.*—Neither this organization, its executive board, or the county and district advisory committees, or any of their executive boards shall have power or authority to incur expenses or make any financial agreements or contracts which shall in any way obligate the State of North Carolina or the United States Department of Labor. No debts shall be incurred by this committee or its executive board or by any county or district committees or their respective executive boards unless previously provided for.

ART. XII. *Amendments.*—Amendments may be made to this constitution by two-thirds vote at a regular and duly called meeting of this committee, provided such amendment shall have been previously approved by the governor of North Carolina and the United States Department of Labor.

APPENDIX III.

CONSTITUTION OF THE NEGRO WORKERS' ADVISORY COMMITTEE OF OHIO.

ARTICLE I. *Name.*—The name of this organization shall be the Negro Workers' Advisory Committee of Ohio.

ART. II. *Purpose.*—The purpose of this committee shall be to study, plan, and advise in a cooperative spirit and manner with employers of labor, with Negro workers, and with the United States Department of Labor for the securing of additional opportunity for employment to Negro labor and greater production in industry and agriculture for winning the war through increasing regularity, application, and efficiency, through improving the morale of Negro workers, and through improving their general condition.

ART. III. *Membership.*—The membership of this organization shall be composed of not more than 30 persons, men and women, of Ohio. At least 5 members shall be women. The chairmen of the council of defense, the Federal director of the United States Employment Service, the Federal director of the Public Service Reserve shall be ex officio members. The governor of Ohio shall be honorary chairman.

ART. IV. *Executive board.*—There shall be an executive board of nine chosen from the general committee. At least two members of the executive board shall be women.

ART. V. *Appointments.*—The members of the committee and of the executive board shall, upon the recommendation of the excutive board and the indorsement of the Federal State director of the United States Employment Service for Ohio, be appointed by the Secretary of Labor, who shall also designate the chairman and the secretary. These officers shall serve for both the advisory committee and the executive board. Thereafter, one-third of the membership of the committee and its executive board shall be appointed every six months to serve for a term of 18 months. Upon the first appointment one-third of the members of both the advisory committee and its executive board shall be appointed to serve until January 1, 1919. The chairman and secretary shall serve for periods of six months each, subject to reappointment. Membership on the committee may be vacated on recommendation by a vote of two-thirds of the committee.

ART. VI. *Meetings.*—Section 1. The State advisory committee shall meet at least once every six months and at such other times as the executive board may decide. Fifteen members shall constitute a quorum.

Sec. 2. The executive board shall meet at least once in every two months, and at such other times as the chairman and secretary shall decide, unless otherwise ordered by the board. Five members shall constitute a quorum. The chairman shall be required to call the meetings of the executive board upon the written request of five members of the board.

Sec. 3. The meeting place of the advisory committee and the executive board shall be the State capitol, unless otherwise ordered by the executive board and approved by the Department of Labor.

ART. VII. *By-laws.*—The executive board shall make such by-laws and rules for the conduct of its business as seem best, not inconsistent with this constitution.

ART. VIII. *Powers of the executive board.*—The executive board shall transact all business, make plans, enter into agreements, and perform such other acts as may be necessary for carrying out the purpose of this committee. All such transactions, plans, agreements, or acts shall be subject to revision by the advisory committee and the United States Department of Labor, through its duly authorized representatives.

ART. IX. *County committees.*—The executive board shall nominate for each of the counties in the State, having in their judgment a sufficient Negro population, a county Negro workers' advisory committee of not more than 11 persons. These persons so nominated are to be appointed by the Department of Labor upon recommendation of Federal State Director of the United States Employment Service for Ohio.

ART. X. *Community committees.*—The State advisory committee may form community advisory committees for localities in their respective communities where the Negro population and local labor problems justify such community advisory committees. The community advisory committees shall cooperate in every practical and honorable way with the county labor boards.

ART. XI. *Finances.*—Neither this organization nor its executive board, nor any county or community advisory committee, nor any of their executive boards shall have power or authority to incur expenses or make any financial agreements or contracts which shall in any way obligate the State of Ohio or the United States Department of Labor. No debts shall be incurred by this committee or its executive board or by any county or community committee or their respective executive boards unless previously authorized.

ART. XII. *Amendments.*—Amendments may be made to this constitution by a two-thirds vote at a regular and duly called meeting of the general committee, provided such amendment shall have been previously approved by the executive board and the United States Department of Labor.

APPENDIX IV.

CONSTITUTION FOR THE NEGRO WAR WORK COMMITTEE OF KENTUCKY.

ARTICLE I. *Name.*—The name of this committee shall be the Negro War Work Committee of Kentucky.

ART. II. *Purpose.*—The purpose of this organization shall be to study, plan, and advise in a cooperative spirit and manner with employers of Negro labor, with Negro workers, and with the United States Department of Labor in securing from Negro laborers greater production in industry and agriculture for winning the war through securing wide opportunity for work, through increasing the morale of Negro workers, and through improving their general efficiency and condition; to promote the production and conservation of food in conformity with the plans of the Food Administration and Department of Agriculture; to promote the work of the Red Cross, Liberty loans, and other war activities.

ART. III. *Membership.*—The membership of this committee shall be composed of not more than 30 persons, colored men and women of Kentucky. At least six members shall be women. The committee on Negro organization of the Kentucky Council of Defense, the Federal director of the United States Employment Service, the Federal director of the Public Service Reserve, the Federal food administrator of Kentucky, the director of farm extension in Kentucky, the chairman of the American Red Cross, the executive secretary of the War Camp Community Service, and representatives of other war organizations shall be cooperating members. The governor of Kentucky shall be honorary chairman.

ART. IV. *Executive board.*—There shall be an executive board of nine, chosen from the general committee. At least three members of the executive board shall be women.

ART. V. *Appointments.*—The members of this committee and of the executive board shall be appointed as follows: One-third of the members of general committee and of the executive board shall be appointed by the Department of Labor; one-third by the Extension Bureau, Department of Agriculture; and one-third by the Food Administration. These members shall be designated also as the committee of the Kentucky Council of Defense for the war work among the colored people. The officers shall be a chairman and a secretary, who will be elected by the executive board. They shall serve for both the general committee and the executive board.

Under the first appointment one-third of the members of both the advisory committee and its executive board shall be appointed to serve until January 1, 1919; one-third to serve until July 1, 1919; and one-third to serve until January 1, 1920. Thereafter, one-third of the membership of the committee and its executive board shall be appointed every 6 months to serve for a term of 18 months. The chairman and secretary shall serve for periods of six months each, subject to reappointment. There shall be a treasurer appointed by the executive board. He shall be under bond for the faithful performance of such duties as the executive board may designate.

143

ART. VI. *Meetings.*—Section 1. The general committee shall meet at least once every six months and at such other times as the executive board may decide.   Fifteen members shall constitute a quorum.

Sec. 2. The executive board shall meet at least once every other month and at such other times as the chairman and secretary shall decide, unless otherwise ordered by the board.   Five members shall constitute a quorum.   The chairman shall be required to call the meeting of the executive board upon the written request of five members of the advisory committee of the board or of both.   The calling of the meetings of both the general committee and of the executive board shall first have the approval of the Negro organization committee of the council of defense.

Sec. 3. The meeting place of the general committee and the executive board shall be Louisville unless otherwise ordered by the executive board and approved by the council of defense.

ART. VII. *By-laws.*—The executive board shall make such by-laws and rules for the conduct of business as may seem best and in conformity with this constitution.

ART. VIII. *Powers of the executive board.*—The executive board shall transact all business, make plans, enter into agreements, and perform such other acts as may be necessary for carrying out the purpose of this committee.   All such transactions, plans, agreements, or acts shall be subject to revision by the general committee, the departments of the Federal Government involved, and the Kentucky Council of Defense.

ART. IX. *County committees.*—The executive board shall nominate for each county of the State having in their judgment a sufficient Negro population a county Negro war-work committee of not more than nine persons.   The persons so nominated shall be appointed by the Departments of Labor and Agriculture, the Food Administration, and the council of defense in the same manner as the State committee and its executive board.

ART. X. *Community committees.*—The county war-work committee may be authorized by the State committee to form community war-work committees for localities in their respective counties where the Negro population and local war-work problems justify such community committees.   This committee and its executive board and the county and community committees shall cooperate with the community labor boards of the Department of Labor.

ART. XI. *Finances.*—Neither this organization, its executive board, nor the county or community war-work committees, nor any of their executive boards shall have power or authority to incur expenses or make any financial agreements or contracts which shall in any way obligate the State of Kentucky or the United States Government.   No debts shall be incurred by this committee or its executive board or any county or community committees or their respective executive boards unless previously provided for.

ART. XII. *Amendments.*—Amendments may be made to this constitution by two-thirds vote at a regular and duly called meeting of this committee, provided each amendment shall have been previously approved by the executive board and the United States departments herein named and by the Kentucky Council of Defense.

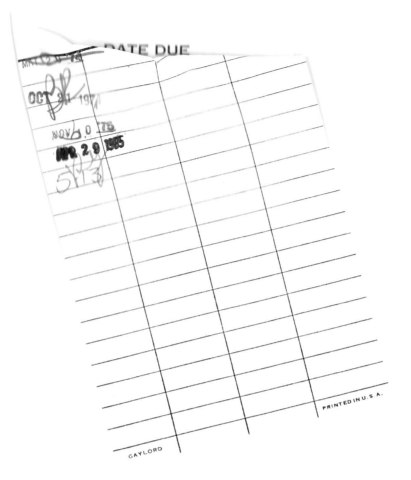

U. S. *Dept. of Labor. Division of Negro Economics.*
    The Negro at work during the World War and during reconstruction; statistics, problems, and policies relating to the greater inclusion of Negro wage earners in American industry and agriculture ₍by₎ Division of Negro Economics. Second study on Negro labor. New York, Negro Universities Press ₍1969₎

    144 p. plates. 27 cm.

    Reprint of the 1921 ed.

    1. Negroes—Employment. 2. European War, 1914–1918—Economic aspects—U. S.   I. Title.

E185.8.U57   1969   331.6′3′96073   70–88453
SBN 8371-1909-X   MARC

Library of Congress   70 ₍3₎